July 2005   Portland, Maine

If you are reading this, you're either thinking of buying t... ... e already shelled out for it. It's our fond hope that you judge it to be a bargain, and pass the word about it.

We started Moon Pie Press in 2003, after we had collaborated with another Maine poet-lawyer, Lillian Kennedy, on an anthology of Maine poetry called A Sense of Place, under the rubric of Bay River Press. When we solicited poets for that book, we received an amazing number of excellent poems. There is a far-flung, extraordinary group of good poets in Maine, plenty of whom have never had a book before. Moon Pie Press has never had to advertise or solicit, but we continue to get a steady flow of wonderful poetry manuscripts crying out to be published. It is our pleasure to get this work out into the world. We think it represents an interesting cross section of poets of differing backgrounds, styles and sensibilities. What we have in common is a love of Maine, which for many of us is an adopted state, and, of course, the drive to craft poems.

Moon Pie Press has grown faster than we ever dreamed it would. As of now, we have thirteen poetry chapbooks out, and several more in the works.   Our press was given a very welcome publicity boost when Garrison Keillor chose four of our poems to read on "The Writer's Almanac" on National Public Radio, in May 2005. (See our website for more on this.)   We called this book "Volume I" because we intend to keep publishing quality poetry, and eventually get a Volume II out there.

We think it's vital to support writers, independent bookstores and the beleaguered arts in general in these difficult times. Thank you again for buying this book, and we hope it brings you great enjoyment. Please stay tuned and check back at our website. (www.moonpiepress.com). We look forward to publishing books by Eva Oppenheim, Marita O'Neill, Dennis Camire, Michelle Lewis, Jay Davis, Patrick Hicks, and other fine poets.

Alice Persons and *Nancy Henry, Co-Publishers, Moon Pie Press*

A Moxie and a Moon Pie:
the Best of Moon Pie Press, Volume I

CONTENTS

DARCY SHARGO (from *The Flame and the Fiction*)

ELLEN TAYLOR (from *Humming to Snails*)

Bad Cat

He was Mr. Sinister Incarnate.
Warpath Cat. Bird–Corpse–Maker.
Evilest of Cats I Ever Had.
I walloped him for dragging
Hot haddock from my plate.
Short–fuse rat–bastard cat

Just sat there & spat:
Hey, man, don't touch
You can feed me,
But I hate you!

Even as a kitten he didn't act right,
As if possessed by an innate malice.
My wife didn't seem to notice—she
Liked him, & how say not too bright
To a sweet mother–love like hers?

He'd shoot from his hidings
Ricochet from room to room
Splurch mouse gobbit vomit
On the beds. Chairs. My shoes.
I wanted him dead, only wished
Him a MacTruck dog collision
With the next door's nasty cur—
BRING ME THE HEAD OF EL GATO
NO QUESTIONS ASKED!

You could see him thinking:
He knew. I knew he knew
I wanted to murder him.
I didn't. It was Gas–
Troenteritis got him
Good. I liked his death.

We poured ammonia on his plot
For offense to all scavengers.
He lies now behind the house.
Wings applaud at the feeders.

He's better off. At rest. No more
Cat-frantic in the closets. No more
Sprayed sofa, clawed Sunday Times,
Cat–turd vendetta whacking my pages,
Surcease of cat-scratch infection.

Unloved, unwanted, death rejoiced,
Easy to hate because he's the cat
Who can't be loved. So awful alive,
& now, poor guy, so awfully dead.
& once I knew he was, then
Of course I missed him.

The Bird My Mother Saw As She Lay Dying

Nights she turns the lights off and tells me stories and this one
takes place in a hospital and everyone has to whisper because
it's about the secret doctors and nurses have always known
how the bird comes when the machines stop
and it's the last thing the dying people see
if anyone else even hints about the bird they could be a goner
they wouldn't be able to live any more they could wrinkle up
they could die like the woolly bears in my mantis feeding jar

Listening I could see it stalking down long white corridors
it was huge it was unfeathered
naked madness and terror shrilling for its lost chicks
and there's this foolish intern and this new nurse
they're saying too much they better watch out
he's asking her did she ever see it no not yet she says
and the visitors tell each other the reek is from the endless hospital days
mixed with the antiseptics and necessaries of the sickrooms
and suddenly there's this closet that no one knew was there
it flies open and inside is scattered what's left of them
the orderly who finds them
he can't stop screaming they have to give him sedatives

> (When I go to look next
> morning hanging on the twigs
> in my mantis jar the woolly bear caterpillars
> are empty sucked out skins)

I heard the witch's icicle-cackle outside the window
I saw her at the apogee nailed to the moon her skirts
streaming fingernails clawing at the clouds
like the witch in my book
O horripilation
even if I cover my ears
mother won't turn the lights back on
in darkness she swears it's true—
the thing in the closet told her
she says she saw the bird
when her own mother died

Should I believe her
Why is she telling me this
She makes me promise to be good
What have I done to earn my fear

                *   *   *

In a past I chose for a present
I tried to ignore the bird.
Mother died in the small days of winter
Her last moments I woke from my doze
I saw her eyes open inside her coma...

        (How to tell the next thing?
        There is some sanity here
        & I will try hard to find it):

I wanted to see what she was seeing.
I wanted to know the way she knew.
I wanted to see the bird she saw.
I got up from the chair.
I leaned against the door.
I felt the bird pass through
the door through me. She
lifted her stare. I saw
what she was seeing.

The bird hopped onto her chest.
Breasts that nursed me went flat.
It dipped its beak into her mouth.
It cawed deep in her throat.
It left hollows in the sheets.

All my life, a fist exploding
inside me I think about the bird.
But it doesn't make me good.
I am the Master of Suspicions.
I open closets inch by inch.

Torture, with Eggs

Every night they snore the house down in their separate rooms
Sans respite & as if for spite & every morning my mother
& my father at breakfast & every morning she'll ask him
What he wants & every morning he'll say You know what
I want I want the usual & she'll say It's every morning
The same thing with you with the juice & the oatmeal
& Sanka & your two toasts with the grape jelly
For God's sake! you smell Like Quaker Oats

Why won't you ever try anything new & he'll say Because it agrees with me
& she'll say Well I don't agree with *you you're always* highly constipated
Every morning you're in there grunting it's like someone's killing a pig
& he'll say Your fault you always forget to add the bran to my cereal
& she'll say Maybe if you tried something new you would like it
& he'll say I am not trying & I am not liking leave me alone
& she'll say O, go ahead I don't care it's your stomach
Do whatever you like. I'm making you eggs.

& he'll say You know some people might just call it being independent
Besides I know what I like & she'll holler *I* am not *some* people
Maybe *you* are *some* people & no you do not know what you like
Supposing your oatmeal people went out on strike then what
& he'll say Save your voice you win & she'll say O please
Just don't do me any favors & now he's conciliatory
You said something about eggs make me an egg
& she'll say But you don't like eggs.

& he'll say Yes I hate them eggs taste funny to me & she'll say
Eggs taste funny to you? So you'll chuckle while you eat
How would you like your egg & he'll say You're the cook
You decide I can't decide & she'll yell It's *your* belly
Do you want fried you want boiled you want poached
You want scrambled or maybe you would prefer it
Cracked on your head just tell me how!!
I CAN'T DAMNIT STAND IT!!

& he'll say OK give me fried & she'll scream
You want FRIED O my God all that grease
You'll be in there again the whole night
Squealing like it's the world ending
& nothing to show for it after
I'm making you oatmeal
The same as I do
Every morning.

I Took Her Hand in Mine

~ for my mother

I took her lank hand in mine,
And only then became aware
A lifelong hate was spent
And I was clasping love.

She was ninety
Letting go of the world
There would be no time
Left to tell her this—

This almost impostor
Who lay dying in her bed,
Her breasts gone
Her smile in the drawer

With the rings
Her fingers were too thin
To bear, and my remorse
Too thick.

His Beautiful Woman

What life is there, what delight,
Without soft golden Aphrodite.
                        ~ Mimnermus (c. 650—c. 550 BC.)

You mean the one with the narrow hips?
    —No, with the broad ones.

The woman he says is always the same?
    —Yes, always same: always new.

The one he calls a woman for all seasons?
    —Her seasons are warm, soft, moist, kind, clear.

The tea rose scented Modigliani thighs woman?
    —Yes, who plants a garden in his beard.

Whose beauty he says she wears like it is natural?
    —No, more like something she has earned.

Perhaps like flower that's won some sort of prize?
    —*Prize* is, well, *obvious* is not quite the word—but yes.

With hair of a fragrance only of hair?
    —No, rosaceous, curls about her, spanks the air like wet fireworks.

The woman he stares at when she leans toward the mirror?
    —Yes, at twin smiles of her female bottom plump as scent bottles.

Otherwise he never stops what he is doing to just gaze at her?
    —He steals side glances, at the movies, when they drive.

The woman he said he didn't want first time he saw her?
    —No, wanted her then. wants her even more now.

But the woman he never shows his poems?
    — No, it's for her he writes them.

Ticket to Ride

~ After Lars Gustafsson

This ticket entitles the holder
To request a seat in first class.

This ticket does not entitle him
To receive one.

This ticket entitles the holder
To travel at the speed of dark.

This ticket does not guarantee the holder
Welcome on arrival. Or arrival.

This ticket guarantees the holder
A precarious tranquillity.

This ticket allows the holder to exit
At any time & without notice.

This ticket does not entitle the holder to love utterly
Accompanied by violins, fine food, or soft berth.

This ticket says "Have a nice day
Unless you have other plans."

This ticket says,
"That's the ticket."

Language as a Second Language

I rushed tingling to the men's room where I sat blissfully
copying her words to my notebook after my Bronx cousin
had spritzed across the restaurant: "*Hey, you, waideh!*
Where's the wawdeh that I orduhed for my dawdeh!
Someone could shrivel up & bust of thirst in here."
Awesome, I thought, that any language could be
so fraught with such exuberant fraughtage.

Nowadays it is the nuggeted poetry
of my neighbor Ernie Pratt I envy
& scribble down, that Down–East
Maine–speak: if I say Nice day,
Ernie, how he drawls back, Yep,
but when them clouds bust
it's gonnuh po-uh buckits!

Another time & place words flowed from an urban spigot.
Here, far from the seltzer of the city, I am the cause
of mirth in others—over 20 years, & for as long as
I am living here, I still can't pass: what gets lost
in any good translation is translation. As for me
Maine remains a second language, as English did
for Conrad & Nabokov—Oh yeah, I only wish!

So I'm in the Gardiner diner & when the waitress says
You from New York City, right? I fake big surprise,
say Bronx, howcudja tell? She says she just knows
when I open my mouth & out comes a *cuppacawfee*

Yeah, I say, but. really, can'tcha tell me how'dja know,
so she gives me: You are not the only one can talk
New York Smartass. The next booth guffaws, so
I shut up that mouth, that only loves & wants
to speak for everything it hears speak to it,
& licks its chops for the sunshine of things
served up in words: it's what a poet does,
no matter where. & that was long ago
the job I signed on to do for life.

Listening to Archangelo Corelli in New England *

Being served dry
biscuits and a watery instant
(bread and water hospitality)
in his New England home
ain't my New York
Jewish dish of tea idea.

Upright, I think, a bit
up-tight, his posture is
a New England tradition
in leather chair with pipe

not anxious like me,
my restless feet marking
itchy time
like the Diaspora.

Maybe he's inside his shoe
tapping time to the allegro,
Archangelo's wings beating
wide over our two worlds.

* Baroque composer Archangelo Corelli (1653-1713)

Bad Poem

~ for Virginia who does not sing like a frog.

Bad Poem verses the page
It's the qualm before the form
Bad Poem's hands are over a barrel
Bad Poem is up a tree without a paddle
Divided against himself he cannot stanza

Bad Poem takes a turn for the verse
He reverses he takes a turn for same
He pulls all the whine out of the violins
If at worst he does succeed sigh sigh again
His prose by any other name would smell as feet

Bad Poem will cross his feet when they come to him
Bad Poem says his whole is greater than the bum of its farts
He says a watched po(e)t never toils & the verse is yet to come
He says I sing like a frog yet I have a beautiful song in my heart
This is the bottom line.

Losing It

You won some lost some—
Lost some winsomeness
Down the drain with
Sum of teeth & hair
That look of young

Your time to use or lose it lost
Lost your way along the way
Thrown for a loss you lost
All sense of what you lost
Found you had

Became the see—er & unseen
You got lost in thought
Lost train & track of
Everything you think
You thought & think

No time left for you to lose
You'd try to find but knew
How again you'd only gain
One more thing for you
To lose anew

You're completely at a loss for words
If your loss wasn't screwed on tight
Bet you'd lose that too
You'd be at a total ...

Hier Ist Kein Warum *

But because he gassed the children
There's got to be a why, an understanding,
Some undermeaning, subsense, a because
To speak to the unspeakable.

Was it only just perhaps because
He was just a man like you or me—
A doctor, husband, father?
Or was it just because perhaps
He was not a man like you or me?

Or does some reason smolder
Just beyond the range of explanation
And there is nothing more to say
Nothing to imagine
Nothing to exhume
No final solution
No mystery after all?

It comes out at the trials:

When he is with his family
He tries to be a good husband and good father
When he is a doctor he tries to be a good doctor
And when it is time for bestiality
He tries to be a good beast.

* Primo Levi recorded his early consternation, during his "first long day in
limbo", when an Auschwitz guard responded to his queries about why he was
not allowed to break off an icicle to slake his thirst with the announcement,
Hier ist Kein Warum (Here there is no why.)

Frogs, Beans, Neanderthals, Frogicidal Princesses

~ for Fran & Donna

Donna says men are like parking spaces: all the good ones taken
the rest handicapped, or too small. & Fran loves that one about
A princess who refuses the frog's kiss, has him killed, cooked,
& eats him, chuckles to herself: *No, I don't fucking think so!*

Donna compares her ex to a jumping bean: his active character
Imparted by an inner worm, a moth larvae, enclosed in nutty
Exoskeleton, ticking away like some bitsy antsy vegetable
In his little dark shell. "& then when you go to open him?
No one home, he's out of there, found someone younger
Got right to it, busy producing a new generation
Of jumpers. A fucking Neanderthal by training,
Now all of a sudden he's monogamous & hard
Working, never goes any place without her,
He's great in bed, improved his posture,
& personal stinky hygiene, Chris'sake,
That used to make her crazy, treats
The new one like a goddamn queen.
Little Prick even cooks for her!"

Since the divorces, if Fran & Donna visit
They always speak past me, to my wife.
Today when they ask me what I think,
I look away, embarrassed:

Myself, a bean in recovery, I really can't speak
For other beans with any degree of confidence,
Everyone is different from me, (& so am I)—
I think they need to ask some other beans.

"Oh we have," they cry, "know what we get?
Mañana! Mañana!! with the bean stares."
"So many frogs," sighs Donna!
"& so few recipes," says Fran!

The Power of It

Ruth woke sad today. Life, she says,
Has been behaving itself & hopeful
Expectations continue, so why now
Nameless dread & mope at sunrise?
What is it? What can it be?

I do not know but I will try.
To help her against it
—whatever it is
I put my arms around her,
Tell her, "What it is, is
There will come moments
When it is simply it."

I say this for myself
As much as for her—
That it is just it.

& it helps.

Untitled

The year was 1937, the place
the front porch of a run-down house
on a back road in a small town in
Aroostook County Maine.
A little girl, four years old
came to the screen door,
scratching the back of her leg
with the front of her other foot.
A tall man had driven up to the house,
crunching the grit of the driveway under the wheels
of an Oldsmobile the size of generosity,
the color of redemption, to bring
the little girl a kewpie doll, and to tell her
he was her father.

This was turning into a promising day for the girl,
the doll being nearly as nice a gift
as having a father and not so equivocal.
(The little girl would not see the tall man
again for almost ten years, and then
only because she made the trip to Portland
to ask for money to help with school
which did not seem like asking too much
of a man who drives an Olds.)

For now, the little girl would hold her prize,
each day, as she scampered out of the way
of the bad-tempered man of the house,
and kept an eye on the new baby, and let
her Mommy know when dinnertime
came so they could eat. And she had
this father, this tremendous thing!
This prize which has the most value for a child
from whom it has been stolen in the first place.
(And he didn't help her with her school,
my grandfather didn't, and curse him for it.)

Knives, or the Way to a Man's Heart

It's been a great couple of weeks for staying
home and sharpening my knives,
and each one has a perfect edge now.
All this honing has really whetted my appetite.
I feel a keen hunger, for freshly
chopped and diced and
julienned and sliced and
shoestringed and French cut and
coarsely chopped and minced
meat and vegetables,
filets of fish and beef and chicken,
carrots, celery, blanched broccoli and
fresh onions, garlic, peppers sweet and hot
strawberries, peaches, all the tropical fruits,
parsley, thyme, rosemary and
every variety of fresh herbs.
Strop, strop, chop, chop.

If you open a box and drop in
100 mice with one piece of cheese
and one small hole to escape,
and wait for the scratching to stop,
one mouse only will exit the hole,
cleaning his claws against his glossy coat,
grinning in the spotlight, mugging
for the paparazzi and nibbling his cheese.
Sociologists will call him *alpha*,
and Psychologists will call him *self-actualized*,
and Calvinists will call him *resolute* and *pious*.
Dieticians say he's non-lactose-intolerant,
and I suppose Political Scientists will call him the *Voters' Mandate*.
Gamblers will call him Lucky,
and what I'll call him is the Capitalist.

The experiment will come to an end
and the glorious multi-nominal mouse
will have his head snipped off

and disposed of by a blonde lab technician
with sterile rubber coated fingers,
who's interning for the summer
and hates this part of her job the most
and just looks forward to going home,
where her boyfriend will be precisely now
starting to prepare a special dinner
for the two of them—
vegetables and meat,
knives flashing, water steaming,
and oil searing in the pots and pans,
in the kitchen that's every bit as hot as Hell.

There's Safety in Groups

I saw a documentary film in which
a multiple personality woman
is interviewed, and tells
how over the holidays there were gifts
hidden all over her apartment which
her many inner people had bought
for each other. She couldn't look
anywhere or she'd ruin the surprise
for someone. . . blessed, with six or seven
personalities, and all
with the energy and resources
and on good enough terms to buy
each other gifts!

I guess all my personalities live
more circumspect and less
friendly lives, confined though they are
together in my head. I do have to fight
sometimes to be heard through the din
of the voices the man who says "No,
for shame," and another who states
simply, "Who you lookin' at. . . ?" The thinker,
the poet, the child, the lecher, the thief;
they all crowd around inside my head
like a party of narcissists
(who think it would have been
a nice party if anyone else but themselves
had been invited).
When someone from the outside asks,
"What do you think?" I have to pose
the question to that crowd,
who promise to get back to me
with an answer, pretty soon now.

Why I Want That Dump Truck

It sits for sale by the road I drive on every day,
and each day I notice it
tall and solid as a Tonka truck
from my childhood, when it was easy
to desire a dump truck with all its promise
of power, and noise, and something definite to do.

It's gray and squat and plain, with long mudflaps
and a dump body staked way up high to hold
an even higher load of branches or wood, lots
of dirt or leaves, or anything that needs to be moved
from here to there loose in a pile or a heap. A Chevy 50,
probably 2½ tons, whatever that means,

whether it's empty weight or loaded, I've never gotten clear.
You see, I'm not much good at dump trucks,
and haven't been since I was a child. This one,
though, this plain gray steel rig, poised up high
on springs over its double rear wheels, small really,
seems like it could be learned and not too intimidating.

For some jobs a dump truck's the only tool that's right.
I have so many jobs now, and though none are
precisely the type that calls for a dump truck,
I want, for once, to know I have exactly
the tool I need at the right time finally
to get the job done, if one of those jobs comes along.

Double Negatives

I've learned nothing from psychology
I've not been able to hold against myself
at one time or another (the grammar checker
in Word hates it, that I said it that way!).
Always selling more than it can deliver,
psychology is the marketing department
of the soul. And the soul always available,
twenty-four/seven, with a mouse click, on ME-dot-com.

Once I wanted only two things: community
and predictability. I tried to be a non-conformist
like everybody else. With age I find the world
is getting more predictable, but the predictions
are worse overall. And now I get this, the advice
that self-loathing is just another form of self-indulgence.
Every anger wants its object to be the biggest,
baddest hombre in Dodge. Listen to anyone
talk about their divorce, or former boss,
or grubby childhood. A regretted past lingers
and influences much longer than a cherished one.
Are you angry about this yet?

For now I've grown to mistrust my rage,
and how the truth keeps changing her mind.
My therapist seems capable of simultaneously
accepting and dismissing whatever cockamamie
thought or scheme I propose. Sometimes the only
reason I get out of bed is so she doesn't think
I'm depressed. My pet wasps have turned on me
again. I'm telling no one. I can't risk not being wrong.

Potatoes

A family of potatoes lives under my sink.
They huddle there like wretched immigrants
in the hold of my kitchen, eyeing anyone
who peers down there with suspicion.
Despite the language barrier, they persist.
The more industrious put down roots.
They wear the same brown shabby coats
they brought from the old country,
though one or two are wrinkled now
from sleeping in them every night.
When the cupboard door is closed
I sense them in there, huddling closer,
muttering in their dark dialect, comforting
one another, whispering their dreams.

When I Die, Mrs. Earnhardt Won't Be Able to Keep the Autopsy Photos Out of the Papers

When I die, I want my autopsy pictures
to be collectors' items on the Internet. E-bay
will have to close the bidding occasionally because
their servers can't keep up with the demand.
An unruly rabble of believers will hijack my body
and tear it apart and run away with it,
and stash all the pieces into little pickle jars,
and wherever the jars are stored will be a site
of miracles, and publications, and bookstores.
There's a poem in my pancreas, you see,
and stories under my skin. I've closed my eyes
and dug for metaphor so often there are little clots
of simile like dirt under each of my fingernails.
Every poem I ever thought about and forgot to write down
is right here, stuck in my throat, trapped
in my lungs, or lying folded and neat in the skull basin
under my brain. Unpublished book reviews are stuck
in my joints like arthritis. And you know where
the love poems are. I want graduate students to interrupt
their studies in order to search out technical gurus
with whom they will spend 1.7 times 10 to the 238th
processor years breaking the strong encryption on my email box
so they can enhance their thesis with some new nugget
of my writing. And they will pass their exam, and get tenure, and thrive.
My body is the Alexandria library all written and transcribed
by just one monk. And all that work will see the light
of day then. Fifty trillion cells of me, and each of them
is a word, a line, a paragraph. And each grisly glob of flesh is a treatise.
Every drop of blood and saliva and tears is a poem that glistens
with love. My bones are archaic poetic forms. Crack them open
and there's hip-hop, and digger, and beat, and bop. My eyes
will delight the imagists, my cerebrum will startle language poets,
my mouth will make the slammers listen. I'm holding my pen
like a knife now. The page is shredding. It's the middle of the day
and my pen is shredding the page and all fifty trillion
of my cells are reciting. I'm alive. Who needs paper?

New Purchase

The count is short, the package
shabby and shopworn
and I'm waiting
for the contents
to settle
due to normal handling.
It seems I've bought some wisdom
at the terrible price of age

Open Reading

Yup, they show up,
to all the readings, every
week, every month. They
have their poem all
wrote out on that flat-
tened out piece of paper,
*"here-in-one-of-these-
pockets*-here. Yeah! Well,"
"Hi, this poem is about my
boyfriend/girlfriend/
father/mother who. . . well. . .
I'll just read the poem,
I know it's long what?
I don't know about time
limits. Just listen. . . I'm shaking
because I've never done this."

Victim, victim,
I got
fucked,
fucked,
fucked
everywhere,
by every-
one,
since day one,
and all
the way
to right
now,
can you
believe it?
That fucker.
"Thank you for your attention"

And the page gets folded
back into the former pocket
and our open poet takes
their dudgeon back
to their table as the next

poet ascends the podium,
and then they're still
nervous I guess,
or feel a draft

because now they're putting
on their coat? And stand-
ing up? And heading for the
bathroom? No? The
door? They're leaving?

After I listened to their unformed
free-associated whining
without a trace of beauty
or dignity or generosity?

Well, at least now that poem
is finished, as the door closes
behind them, and I know
finally how it feels
to be them, and fucked.

Homework

I looked you up in the dictionary of love.
You're an adverb, meaning absent.
The index referred me to Volume 3
but the dictionary is only two volumes.
Volume 1 is entitled yesterday.
Volume 2 is entitled today.

The Thesaurus says you're gone
or waiting in the same place leaves
on the tree stay in winter.
It says my love lives
in the place where infants wait
before they're conceived.

I almost sense where you are.
You're there, where addiction goes,
when the substance disappears.
I hear you in overtones and harmonics.
You're an echo inhabiting the space
between the walls of the empty rooms

in which I wait to hear your voice. I think
you're the last stanza of my next poem.
You're sitting in the front row of the classroom
across the hall facing away. I drove past you
last night while asleep at the wheel.
I hope you're the punch line to this joke.

Dear Barbie

Here, eat, I've made you some salad.
Watercress and walnut oil, but just
a little. . . I know how hard it must be
to keep up your diet, and stay

looking the way you do. Your legs,
so impossibly long, bring me to
remember the first time I saw you
without your clothes. It's when I knew
I wanted to grow up.

Your insouciant optimism inspires me,
as well as how good you look even
as you pass your fortieth birthday!

You're an inspiration for me to put
on a pressed shirt in the morning
and find a tie with nice colors. Today
I want to look good, and maybe
you'll notice me.

I'll never be impolite in your presence,
and you're the only woman who could
ever make me consider quitting smoking.

You'd do well to ditch Ken, that pig,
who I've heard now wants to get
to know Skipper. And he has other
questionable qualities, too. I actually
found the guy in my daughter's room
dressed up to party in *your* clothes!

I'm glad you don't let it bother you
that so many women shun you
for being shallow and vain,
and the men think you're stupid.
We know better, don't we. . . let them talk.

I'll give you what you deserve, the benefit
of the dignity and respect that forty years
of being with the kids entitles you to.
Marry me, Barbie.

Pure Poem

I've taken all the nature out of this poem.
It's not necessary. I'm tossing out the flowers
and trees, and the birds that live in them,
and the season, and any other item which may
cause associations unintended by this poem.
And now that we're getting into it,
I'm going to take away any reference
to another time, because nostalgia
may not be in this poem; we've no need
to hold to any past comfort. I will have
very few people in my poem, none
certainly whom I might offend by accident,
so I may avoid speaking in a politically
correct manner. There's no need for
geography or regionalism I think,
as it's only you and me standing here
on the edge of this nondescript cliff
overlooking the great abyss, admiring
its depth, our great height over it, and knowing
how exposed and helpless our position, clinging
to the sheer wall, so that when you suggest
we might jump to defy the status quo,
I say "sure, let's jump," and fully intend to do so,
but not just yet, and right after you.

Fuchsia

Last Wednesday I brought home
a big, glorious fuchsia plant,
three feet across and effervescent
with blossoms, pendulant with buds-
to hang off the porch outside my kitchen door-
loving the flowers and feeling the spring,
wanting that pink and promiscuous display.

On Friday afternoon, I discovered
a silly and hedonistic couple, barn swallows-
who must have thought they'd died and gone to
Niagara Falls had built their nest
of love right there in that hanging pot,
with flowered ceilings and walls--loving
in that gaudy and fragrant honeymoon suite

How to Write A Poem

First, forget about the words. They'll come
and take care of themselves. Forget
big subjects because they'll just get in the way.
Let's say you want to write about the biggest
fear you've got. . . something that makes you
mute on just imagining it. That's your subject.
But don't write about it. Write about a mouse
that eats then scurries across the floor
of the kitchen, knowing anytime it could be killed
by the kitchen's owners, but knowing that hunger
can kill as well. Name the owner of the kitchen Fear.
Name the hunger Desire. Eat. Watch.
Run when necessary. Give the mouse your name.
Pull the paper on which these words are written
off the desk, across the floor, through a tiny hole
near the baseboard. Build a nest that's lined with shreds
of paper. Raise your babies inside this warm place.
Expect the worst. Fear lives just outside.
Desire will always bring you closer to Fear.

Indian Silence

The reservation road was empty
when Jeff pulled over and cut the engine.
Stillness rang down the Black Hills, earth humming
like woods when you've cut your chainsaw.

The hawk lay dead on the sandy shoulder.
Jeff slipped out a knife, glanced along the road
and cut off its beak and claws.
I took four brown and gray streaked feathers.

I was careful with those feathers, hitchhiking
and riding the Greyhound back to New York.
In the clamorous Brooklyn days,
I remembered that Indian silence.

> sun in bright cloud
> yellowing the sandy earth
> hum of razor wings

When Brett began making masks
for fashionable up and down-towners,
I gave him those feathers and told him where they came from.
He gave them back in a hawk's mask, streaked with gold.

I hung the mask on the remains
of an ornate mirror I found in the trash.
I moved to Maine, Brett died from AIDS.
Gold beak jutting under cloudy mirror eyes.

It's November now, gold in the witch hazel, sun
glaring from cloud, its bright circle sliced by razor wings.
Too bright for me, like a god unmasked.
Earth hums underfoot, shadow of wings on gray rock on Bald Mountain.

Under the Autumn Clear Sky

1

Those who say the God
who men remember
is only the work of mens' minds
and does not in turn remember them
seem able to live in a world
where men may no longer remember.
I try to live in that world,
but thought will trap the thinker
as the Labyrinth did its mythic builder.
Some fly like birds, and escape.
I'm earthbound.
Sometimes walking will ease my mind.
That and a song, a simple song
of the rose and silver moon.
And a prayer, for protection
against loneliness,
against trapping God
in the mind.

2

Walking, under the autumn clear sky.
Smoke through bare branches
passing like prayer, into the wind.
Ducks pressing the wind, calling.
Car tracks showing the road.

The Hasidim say that during the month of Elul
the King is in the field, among the people.

Walking, over the frosted rail ties,
steel rails freezing the sun.

Woods give way to field,
corn stalks cut low are brown and cracked,
dull gray earth hard with ruts.
Barbed wire strung through cedar posts.

Elul came late this year,
frost early, pale as a corpse.

Walking, under the autumn clear sky,
waiting.
For the ducks to fly back?
Barbed wire to soften?
For a prayer to take hold.
To be held again.

Note: In Jewish tradition, which runs on the
lunar calendar, Elul is a month of introspection

The Kapishnitzer Rebbe Rules on Business

Louis Leib climbs to America
in a boat. He is twelve,
he has six dollars, he speaks no English.
He works in his uncle's grocery,
and never sees his parents again.
He opens his own store,
when the bank asks for collateral
he points at his chest.
He marries under a tenement sky.
He saves money and invests in sugar.
Sugar is sweet, the cost is high.
It too is coming to America in a boat.
The boat is very slow.
The price of sugar drops.
The price of sugar hits a record low.
When they go to bed, Louis doesn't tell Sarah
they are losing their savings.
He dreams he is drowning.
His father hauls him out of the water.
Louis gasps. He feels his father's cracked finger
On his salty lips:
Shhh. You should not worry.

The next evening, while Sarah tells Louis
she had to hide Herbie from the fish peddlar
after he spread catnip all around the wagon,
Louis reads in the paper that the sugar boat sank.
Insurance covers his loss and then some.
Louis buys stock.
Stocks go up. Louis is rich.
They crash. Louis is poor.
Germans pave the street in his Polish village
with stones from family graves.
Louis starts a business in hardware.
Soon he has a warehouse full of fasteners.
Two Puerto Rican men ask him for a loan
to open a shop to cut hair.
From the ink-stained pocket in his rumpled shirt
Louis pulls a wad of bills
in a greasy rubber band.

Herb laughs. "That's a lot of money, Pop,
You just lost."
"What lost? They will repay it."
"Right. No contract, not even an IOU—
Pop, why'd you give him your money?"
"He had an honest face, that one."
Louis is angry at Herb
because Herb won't pray in the synagogue
or visit the Rebbe.
Herb says Louis is superstitious.
Herb and Louis disagree—about business.
Louis says, "We will ask the Rebbe then."
"The Rebbe? Pop, you give him money every holiday,
he knows I'm not even kosher—
of course he'll side with you!
Besides, what does *a rabbi* know about hardware?"
"Anyway, we'll ask."

The two men return to pay back the loan
with interest.
Herb humors Louis, drives him to Henry Street
on the Lower East Side.
The Rebbe listens, stroking his beard.
He says, "Louis, in this matter,
your son is correct."
Louis thanks the Rebbe.
Later, he will take his grandchildren there
for a blessing,
the blue ink
staining the pocket of his white shirt
like old blood,
marking his heart.

Feathers

A pile of feathers grounded
under a leafless maple

once so sagely ordered, now a splayed circle
randomly pointing the six directions.

Some memory of the old architecture holds them
against the scatter-hungry wind,

groups of three or four, clumped at the quills,
held by what's left of the flesh they once warmed.

These feathers are common gray save the few smallest,
tipped with purple, dancing like baby tadpoles.

The wind will have them soon, quick fingers
on a keyboard racing down budding boughs.

Branches wag at spreading cloud, drawing me upward
from the dead to the gathering sky:

A hawk's been circling here lately,
scanning naked woods for dancing purple.

Black and Yellow: Part I

G
Maple branchlet finger, peels moist, cuts clean.
Brown burn lines fashion turtle, hawk, cat, bear—
hard tan beads.
It was the fox bones drove me.

C
I had a canoe once, backside of a guitar for a paddle.
Lake slapping rocks, I tied off near somebody's fire-ring
and walked over ties sticky with tar.
Tried to balance on the rail till losing the rhythm.

I placed a buffalo head down
with the same touch it takes to find one harmonic.
Heard they were all gone, maybe I could stretch one
into memory.

Train came, crushing my coin, tracks bobbing underneath.
Indian head so flat it could strum my guitar, or slice my finger.

A bit down the line, a skeleton—
small bones shining between the rails
like ivory eyes on the neck of a fiddle.

G
No flies buzzed those sun-warm bones,
but butterflies, black and yellow,
flitting among the ribs, caressed them.

I thought it might collapse
but the skeleton held, between two sticks,
bearing the bones up to pale grass.

The butterflies all scattered,
save one, stuck between the ribs.
Worried I'd crushed it
but, folding wing over bone,
it slid across a rib, vibrating
like string under a bow—

paper thin, notes turning to air,
it flew up the heliostat rail.

Midnight, P-Ridge

Along the dark road
I feel the fields silent
and invisible beckon
with soft bedding,
breezes, willing earth.
Is it the wind or your spirit
brushing my cheek?
What's been gripping me lately
gently paralyzing, disorienting,
seems to blow in like dark clouds
or locust, silently over the fields,
something seasonal, almost planetary.
High in the southern sky
glowing, like a red gemstone
lit with yellow back-light,
Mars gleams, not angrily as in the myths
but puzzled, maybe at the wars
battering earth's orbit.
Outsized orange half-moon
caught among treetops—I'm sick
of unreachable beauty, sick
of gravity and my own fixed
broken orbit—once, if cut free
I would have panicked, now
I'd simply stretch until I reached you
floating by, one more shooting star.

One More War

I

Empty me! Empty me!
The cows' bellow cutting through tractor roars.
Aussie Mike wanted to work in the Kibbutz dairy
but they were full up as their cows' udders at milking.
Meanwhile he was chasing chickens—
lunchtime he'd settle on a table and everyone there move away.
I was picking artichokes in the winter rain,
lifted my face to a hot shower and saw an artichoke spouting water.
The harvest ended and I had to check the board each day for my job.
One morning, over coffee and cucumbers, Mike said,
"Just got the word? I'm moving to the dairy?"
Almost everything Mike said sounded like a question.
"Maybe you oughtta take over for me? With chickens?"
Chickens, Mike?
"Beats looking at the board each morning?"

First, scrub the blue feeders and red waterers in witches' brew,
soap bubbles' chemical purple popping in the morning sun.
Fresh chips smelling of trees for chicks trucked in the day they were
born.
Lights dim, quiet now, or they'll hear you and think you're their mother.
Last, pack the squawking birds for the slaughterer,
empty me
suddenly silent on the idling truck.

Tree-tall Dovid ruled the two large lools, eyeing his birds
and workers like an osprey staring down a pond for fish.
Captain in the '73 war, Dovid spoke sternly,
and was too fond of his English to teach you much Hebrew,
but he couldn't understand Aussie Mike in either language.

2
Mike had been in the dairy and me in the lool for weeks when Gedaliah
blew in.
Blond peyot and tzitzit flying, white long sleeve shirts, thick lenses—
he even had prescription goggles—unfocused eyes, and stories no one
believed.

One evening, over milk and cucumbers, Mike said,
"That Gedaliah? Lives in your building?
He's been prowling round the refet?"
Prowling, Mike?
"At odd times, yeah? Asking for dead ones?"
Dead ones?
Later, in the library, Gedaliah flinging back the door.
"You got any books on tannin'?"
Asking the librarian, I guess, his eyes somewhere over our heads.

Then, back in our room, Gedaliah lunging through the door,
white sleeves rolled back, arms dripping blood,
smiling.
"Where you been?"
"Skinnin' a calf!"

I glanced at the shower, but Gedaliah liked strolling around covered
with blood.
In the steep August sunlight the calf's blood
made red-gold droplets along his arms.
I felt Gedaliah wanted to strip and smear his body with blood—
sometimes our secret urges and the neighbors' disapproval
are both real as heavy stones perched on a hillside
and the gravity that holds them.

Gedaliah hung five hides on a line near the dairy.
When he figured they were dry he banged out the door
while the sun rose in a reddening sky.
Later he didn't say much, only that the hides were gone.
Then, how he blew up a bridge in Viet Nam,
holding the explosives in place with dead bodies.

3

Yossi ran the little lool.
Semi-retired, he spoke little English.
If you asked Yossi about the war, he'd say,
"Which one?" *World War II? 48? 56? 67? 73?*

He drank coffee, smoked cigarettes,
liked to listen to the radio—but not alone—
so he'd call me in for the news.

Yossi grew up in Poland, stitching clothes in Izhbitz,
and, sometime during the war, moved to Auschwitz.
After liberation he moved back to Izhbitz
looking for missing relatives.

He made good business as a tailor
but too many threads were cut,
too many holes couldn't be patched.

          "No one left alive, I felt like a ghost—
          I went up to Israel."

I never asked Yossi what fighting through five wars was like,
he mostly talked about his kids and grandkids anyway.
          "Hanan got his Class II license."

I did ask once, "Yossi, when you were in the camps,
did you ever pray?"
     He turned down the radio, balanced his cigarette on a saucer.

          "Every day I thanked God
             for each word of the prayers
               that I could remember."

          Hanan got his Class II license.

Aussie Mike married a Yemenite soldier and moved to her village,
the elders nod gently when he speaks, as if they understand him.
Gedaliah unrolled his sleeves in Yeshivah in Jerusalem,
washes his soul in the Mikveh, sits puffing a pipe over Maimonides.
I was travelling when I heard Hanan was killed,
fighting in Lebanon.
I saw Yossi's hand shake, cigarette fall
beside his empty cup.
Heard the cows shriek, the chickens go silent.

note: a *lool* is a chicken barn; *refet,* a dairy; *peyot,* sidecurls worn by some orthodox Jews;
tzitzit, fringes worn on the corners of an undershirt by orthodox Jews;
yeshivah a Jewish religious school; *mikveh* a ritual bath

Black and Yellow: Part II

C
Nubman played the blues.
His remodeled fingers flew so fast down the fretless bass
a fly once dropped stunned at my feet.

He had the 'bo in his blood,
his daddy rode the blinds,
came home on weekends to drink,
teach Nubman the blues, and beat him like a drum.

Nubs said with a capo I could find my own pitch.
I heard those notes on the rail sing through the bones,
ties like frets on a giant two string guitar,
bone and butterfly melody drawing me back.

The next day I counted twelve white teeth
and fourteen missing.
Found a railroad spike, cut the skin holding the jaw,
took the jaw home.
Filed the ends to hold tight with stretched gut,
desire hitched to hunger, straining past clamped jaw.

G
Pulled back the next day,
I searched among rocks between ties.
Windblown waves' lap-rattle-slap beating blues
under blue summer sky, I felt like Nubman's stubs
sliding down the rail, seeking one more note.

Found five sharp teeth—notes dropped across a clef.
Knocked out by the train?
Each tooth had two roots, so just seven had been missing.

Wrapped teeth in tissue, put them against my hip with the bones.
Placed three crushed coins, with a fresh one on top of each
on the track and walked back, full
of lack of ceremony,
so lost in a chorus of thought
the train got close before I heard
its cradle-rock rhythm strumming behind me.

Walking Track

Bright eyes gleam at a rail crossing
the fox paused, as if to say,
>> Come on, walking track beats driving roads
>> on foggy nights.

Fox, I've seen animals dead on the rail—
where are you going?
>> *Come on—*
>> *walking track.*

There's a calm that is living and a numbness that is dead—
who will teach me the difference?
>> *Come on, walking track beats philosophizing*
>> *on foggy nights.*

Eyes dissolve in darkness, where endless tracks disappear.
Fox, which do *you* fear most—life or death?
>> *Come on, walking track—sing the blues, feel the wet breeze,*
>> *look for gleaming eyes.*

The Rebbe of Satmar Visits Jerusalem

Looking over her silver needles as if she were knitting a window,
my Grandmother tells me of the time she saw the Satmar Rebbe
walking on a Brooklyn street.
"I thought, 'this is the holiest man I ever saw—
not even a man anymore, more like an angel he was!'"

      This was the old Rebbe, sailed to America during the war.

Someone else told me, "The Satmar Rebbe visited Israel,
he was sitting on the Bimah, on Yom Kippur, when a man, dressed all in white
rose from the congregation, walked up to him and shouted,
'You left, while your people had to stay—I accuse you—
of leaving your people to die alone!'"

      This was after the SS emptied Hungary,
      the Rebbe taken by train to Switzerland out of Bergen-Belsen.

" *'How could you leave your people behind?'*"

The fellow who told me this went on,
"And the Rebbe listened and said—
                    nothing."

"What does it mean?" I asked him,
                    "This silence?"

note: A *Rebbe* is a revered leader of a Hasidic group
      A *bimah* is an area in a synagogue where those leading the prayers sit.
      Yom Kippur is the Jewish "Day of Atonement"

Light With the Power of a Name

Softly at first, louder if need be,
like the mystics naming God,
if I had a word for your loneliness

I would chant it.
What they named they commanded,
like warriors eating their enemies' hearts.

I, chanting your loneliness till I, too,
am vast and silent as devouring night, relentless
with freedom as icy wind—

chanting the mix of blood and words
some call magic, some poetry,
crescendo some call prayer.

Like the mystics naming supernal beings
to dominate their realms,
if I could name your loneliness,

summon it to exile through syllables
beating like wounded hearts
in broken lines, I could say,

let there be light,
and there would be.
And you would finally see it.

Black and Yellow: Part III

D
Rock, steel, tar,
copper, nickel, wood and the railroad earth.

Got down the canning pot,
built a fire, started boiling the bones.

Flesh tooth skin bone—fur & steam
thick on my skin, greasing the air.

Notes pitched for me
whistled past the pot and between my teeth.

C
Turtle beads of maple,
heartwood cored, strung between small bones

may you be flexible as the fox
for me, patient as the turtle

sun water wind smoke fire
musk dusk dance across the tracks

and somewhere a fox
and a whistling train

wise as the bear
visionary as the hawk

may you be
intuitive as the cat

for me and let me
let me sing my blues.

Ocelot

I think of you bathed in ebony
the tangled garden
blossoming
with some ripe and fragrant flower,
sorrow-bound wings
discarded by love,
musky oils so
false and fragrant
flowing from your soul.
Beloved come to your garden,
strike my silky
flesh with your hot tongue.
Slip out of the pale jade window,
go to the river again
painted in my slippery fluids.
Embrace the world this way,
bathed in the soft amber light,
dance deeper inside
in the momentary glow
of evening.

In/Out

She kisses
his forehead, bids him
to trail hot, wet kisses
down her invisible barrier.

Slowly, he is
becoming incorporeal.
Entering her, he
becomes birds,
poetry, dolphins,
starlight.

Like a tiny buried seed
which sprouts into
rice and corn and maize,
she possesses
a mysterious power.

He has never told her.
She is becoming spirit, and
it's not just the wine.

Eros

Taking his sweater
off the floor,
she slides it
over silken hair
feels its
scratchy warmth
against her shoulders,
breasts,

lifting
winter overalls
all grease and fumes
from the hook
by the cellar door
she leans her cheek
on the rough cloth

making up
their bed
she kneels
face in his pillow

breathes.

An Early Morning

They do not allow us
to look into their faces
but imagine:
stars fading,
the delicate current in her wrist
like the pulse in a green frog's throat,
stains and glories of new love
in the mingled fury of sheets.
Rose petals of her skin,
sea glass of his eyes,
cool dawn light,
kissing each other
out of dreams.
They tangle in one another's thoughts
wandering the island of heart.
Naked in the blue waters
just offshore, they swim together
towards one moment
of passionate union,
forgetting there is more distance
and impossibility in love
than in death itself.

Grave Clothes

In my kitchen, salt whispers to crystal,
the red teapot dreams lightly, ready to wake
at the sudden purple argument of flame.

Lazarus, come,
I am in need of your healed and shining skin,
your fragrant, re-created hair,
your humming cells
radiant with the unmaking of the curse.

I know those dark canyons of hollow ache
where you give your sad face to the stars,
to the wild scent of autumn on the black breeze,
to the slim line of fire above the darkening sea.

These nights you have troubled my dreams,

the ivory plane of your cheek,
sweet limitless pools of your eyes,
your blessed, myrrhed breath,
the taste of the sea on your secret skin.

And You Would Still Be Gone

I can't sleep nights
light cigarettes out of spite
for the wind and the dust of a thousand miles
for the aging widows in sweltering rooms
for the birds hopelessly lost in radiance.
Yes, I do remember when you were with me,
a beautiful hand
unfoldng the blue sheets, two children
sheltered in the moss-covered corners of stone,
observing the barely perceptible rotations of this
world.
South of the river
we sat dreaming the doubters' dreams;
bees saying their morning prayers over the tall grass,
candles burning on the gravestones.
If I could draw that moment back
through that last pearly slit in the night,
then, my sister, from the edge of our high window
I would see battalions of finches
on the shoulders of the reddening trees
all gone beneath the beastly rains of November
like gods fallen out of the sky.

Flight School

The bed reaches out
to gather you in
and all, all your answers
are there in her pillowed arms
the lesson you learn
sprawled in flesh
is to fly or fall
you plead
strain for the soft, moist
mercies of the tongue
sweat
wedded groin hip and thigh
to desire's blind ache
climb the tight pulsed ladder
of muscled bone
clawing for the next wide view of sky
that swallows you
stricken one sharp instant
with a fullness you have never known
for one ragged breath,
ripped free from finitude
you rise in the bright capsule
of this feeling so far
beyond pain
you bite your own fist bloody
to keep from screaming.

What Heart Wants

In her musky chamber
heart longs secretly to be devoured.
Peel her skin back with your teeth
lap her agonized juices with your
languorous velvet tongue.
In fierce, snapping bites
sever sweet filaments tangled in
garnet-jelly seed.
Remember when the heart cries out,
she lies, she longs to be consumed,
is practiced in deception, to distract you
from her true intention. Sit down
at the table, then, and tear into heart
with wolf-like abandon.
Love her broken languages of sorrow,
naming all her fated, grieving colors
even as they burst
upon your tongue.

May

Passion is fishing in your hair
for a strand of that particular light.
She holds a blue pencil
softly wrought with all you need.
Passion is fishing
with a very delicate hook.
She plays fiddle by the graveyard,
wakes the dead,
will not let you bury
any beautiful thing alive.

Jane and Jacob

A gentle form of haunting, this
Kneeling in freezing slush
Before a tilted slate stone
Taking note of light and shadow
Waiting for the shutter click.
Her stone leans gently on the breast of his
Jacob Bradbury, died May 8, 1837
Jane P., wife of Jacob
Died October 2, 1863.
This is all I know.
That they were pledged to one another at some time.
That her stone reclines on his.
In this I discern passion and glory, tragedy and
struggle
Grief.
And finally,
Peace.
The deer are in velvet now
The earth in the flux of melt and freeze
That green wood doesn't throw off much heat
I hear the whispered sizzle of its green blood,
My tea grows cold too soon.
Forecast says
Exercise caution on the highways
Fog is possible in the low-lying areas.
Snow will spread up to Caribou
Around midnight.
It will fall, becoming rain,
Over the shellfish flats
North of Princess Point.

Europe on Five Dollars a Day

In our rented Fiat,
we drove the perimeter of Rome seven times
as the ancient dream grew darker with each tense circling,
gathering indigo dusk around its stone and music.
My unilingual father cursed in English only,
looking for any street that ran both ways.
"All roads lead to fucking Rome, but they won't let you in!" he snarled,
and then we laughed in our exhaustion,
our crazy joy to be circumnavigating this place
that sang and glowed in all our separate dreams:
my father, Michelin phrase book useless in his lap,
my mother wrapped in her big houndstooth
coat, lighting another cigarette,
me, slightly carsick in the back seat, wearing the
smart wool suit my mother sewed for this occasion.
Chill November was off-season, everything a bargain then.
It was midnight before we got to the pensione,
struggled up the stairs with our mammoth
avocado suitcases, our sensible walking shoes
tracking the threadbare path worn in the musty aubergine carpet.
And who needed the warmth and light of the costly summer season?
I had Italy, opening all my doors: first coffee, bittersweet and dark,
first glass of wine, humming with woody mysteries,
first kiss on those shabby stairs from the Tuscan porter,
eyes as blue as the water we viewed from donkeys
gingerly edging along the cliffs of Naples,
as blue as the Virgin's robe in all those crumbling frescoes,
and oh the taste of his firm tongue olives
and chianti while my parents napped
in the yellowish smoggy light of the late Rome afternoon.
Who could notice we were eating mostly
bread and cheese, washing our underpants and stockings in the chipped
communal sinks?
I was thirteen, and all that naked marble made me burn.
I longed to press my just-awakened lips against the David's smoothly
muscled thigh,
cup the milky breasts of headless nymphs
in my warm, aching palms. My diary records:
"Italy is very interesting, we are having fun,
it is cold, we have looked at many churches."
I did not dare to say more,
but I remember.

Anchovy

Oh anchovy
you are the very bacon of fish!
I crunch your crystal filament bones
and suck your extravagant salt
with the gusto I reserve for life's
deepest joys.

Oh wondrous catfood-smelling strip
of rosy needled flesh
you are simply great with beer and olives.
You make my breath a Liverpool fish market.
Eye-watering link to my wandering ancestors
I can take you in a backpack anywhere
your shelf life venerable, for what microbe
dares assail your brine?

Noble minnow
flashing through shallow seas
in silverfire fortresses
you are the legendary "little fish"
of the foodchain.

Select prey of sea lion, eel
and premenstrual woman
we share a king of tide
you sleep in narrow tins
waiting for the moon's dark pull
that draws me barefoot
filled with a midnight lust
just short of madness.

Tea Green

for Harold

College and my manic brother got me drinking tea
Morning Thunder, up all night
in the cinderblock dorm room, hotplate simmering
with heart-pounding brew. I'd write and hyperventilate
'til morning, trying to wrestle Kierkegaard
to the turquoise formica and make him gasp
just one insight from those morose gray lips.
Lost cause. I changed my major after that semester,
then changed it again. Took up coffee.
Learned, a little bit, to fail.
Twenty years are gone, and I say, good for that
their passage brought me you.
You drink green, double-bagging that fierce
antioxidant and caffeine. Watching you make tea is
my sweet tease those ivory spindle fingers;
their tender tremble and that musician's grace.
You woke me one night, twiddling my nipple
through my flannel gown. "I'm sorry,"
you murmured, "I dreamed I was playing
my bass." I'll be your bass, and sing
like that stainless steel kettle
from a belly just that round and hot.
This green, I see in the belly of your white cup
and again in your eyes, crazy
can't-decide-green, this green of rivers
stained with cypress-tannin, a little
grass-snake sneaky green, a flash of
watered-silk turkey feather browngreen.
I was a Bible teacher once.
I remember a few things:
how Jacob got HIS limp,
(a better story than my own);
"manna", approximate translation: "what is it?";
and all the desert colors of a part of Earth
bleached and blazed with the savage gaze of grace.
But green saved for a few strokes of hope:
Galilee, Jordan, rose of sharon;
God's throne, impossibly haloed with emerald rainbow.

What I Really Did On My Summer Vacation 1972

Mrs. Beeler, here's the thing:
I did not go to the beach and collect shells;
I did not ride my bike a lot and have fun.
My sister got knocked up, and mostly I stayed
in my parents bed watching Dark Shadows
with the covers pulled over my head
at the scary parts.
We did not do cookouts at the park.
I made baloney sandwiches every day,
and had to feed the dog everyone else
forgot about.
I found my dad's Playboys
and now I'm pretty sure I'm not actually a girl.
My brother got caught smoking pot,
and Dad broke all his Beatles albums
by running over them in the driveway, with the Jeep
my brother is not allowed to drive anymore.
And guess what, Mrs. Beeler?
I know Laura Corbet is lying about riding horses
and going to summer camp, because she lives next door
and her mother got drunk lots of times and screamed at her dad a lot
and he moved to a hotel and Laura stayed at our house
most weekends and we
painted our toenails and shaved our legs without permission
and stole my sister's cigarettes
and decided not to believe in God.
So do me a favor Mrs. Beeler,
and don't give anyone
this stupid essay next year.

We are lying to you.
You don't know us at all.

Don't think you do.

Raga

I'm dancing naked in front of the big mirror over the sofa
weaving in and among piles of laundry and open
poetry books on the floor
flinging my arms around, moving my hips, wavelike,
trying to make my belly do something that looks come-hither and alluring;
feverishly dancing to the Last Train to Clarksville
on sitar on that weird station I only get here behind the mountain
on a clear day.
I've been reading Rumi, and a book about the goddess within;
I'm making peace with my body; trying to grow more comfortable
with my fat.
It's turned up pretty loud
this rendition of the Last Train to Clarksville
on sitar, my heels are pounding our old floor like frenzied drums
their winter pale oblivious burden moving all directions.
I'm just trying to learn to celebrate my softening body dancing in my new
purple hair—an accident I'm enjoying.
All full of Rumi, I'm communing with my inner goddess:
someone bountiful, someone who will lead the tribe to food
in harsh winter, someone starving men desire.
Like I said it's pretty loud; this is the longest version
of Last Train to Clarksville I have ever heard,
drowning out my neighbor who is calling out my name,
I'm sure, but not too loudly.
This is a small town.
Just as I am noticing how my breasts are bouncing,
wondering if this is a good or bad thing,
and deciding I like the look of it
— there she is with my casserole dish

and she says
she says
excuse me
did I come at a bad time?

Map to Myself

For your safety and convenience, I drew a map to myself, with several alternate routes, all marked. All sights of interest and occasions for caution are indexed and carefully noted in the margins. See the tortured lines around Subterfuge, Insecurities, Hot Buttons. This map comes complete with warning signs in red : Severe Avalanche Danger, Careful Not to Awaken Sleeping Obsessions, Dungeon of Troubling Memories, Vast Pit of Need. I did not forget to mark the attractions, the Sights Not to Be Missed: Bizarro House of Illusions, Library of Revisionist Personal History, Portrait Gallery of Lost Love.

Only up for a nice day trip? Note that on the modern superhighway you can whizz directly to the outskirts of my False Self, very attractive. You can picnic within view of a lovely skyline painted in trompe l'oeil fashion. Do not try to drive into this city, however. Most people choose this route, have a little picnic, snap a photo and drive on home in time for bed.

At the end of the most twisted road, unpaved, rutted, potholed, is the sign "Open Heart: Owner Not Responsible For Damage to Person or Property". If you are an explorer, really up for some punishment, if you have a four-wheel-drive, or better, if you are backpacking in, you may get this far. From that point on, it's uncharted territory. The map ends here with a dragon, a couple of ships plummeting off the face of the earth. You're on your own. Even I have never been there.

Approaching Twilight

On the phone my mother rattles on -
a warm incessant buzz about Louella and her goiter
listing obituaries of friends and former residents
as one by one the doors of The Elms open and close.
The ambulances carry her friends past the cornfield that is her backyard.

After love yous and protracted good-byes
I stand at the window, run my eyes over the maples
and a horse-shaped cloud.
I see her a thousand miles away,
standing in her nightclothes at the screen door -
a small crowd of moths leaves the yellow light of her porch
vanishing into the tasseled stalks.

Overhanging Branches

There are days
when we need the long view
of plains stretching softly to the horizon
or of the sea building and receding from coast
when the world we see must be filled
with sky and possibility,
but here and now with fall pressing,
bare-limbed oaks throw their arms up
and pines fling their longest shadows -
our dreams are confined
to a small tunnel of winter night
and the small singing of the stars
before the coming whisper of snowfall.

The Pencil Farmer

takes off his work jacket,
its dark pockets full of the
unused verbs and dangling participles.

He throws it
disgustedly
at the hook;

heads to the sink
to cool his blistered fingers
in clear well-water;

splashes lead dust from
under his broken nails,
from the creases of his face.

From a shirt pocket he pulls
a damp scrap of paper
the words, "not enough time"...

then stands at the screen
watching fireflies and wishes
early summer evening was another workday yet.

April 23, 1962

On a warm spring Sunday afternoon
Buddy Johnson walks to his garage,
climbs into his 1940 Willys coupe,
coasts down the hill to the long curve
Main Street makes at the edge of town.

He sits a moment, lights a Lucky,
looks up at the picture of Cheryl on the visor
and pushes the starter button:
domed pistons slam fuel toward the heads,
recoil from the explosion, cams twist,
the flywheel spins against the pressure on the brake,
tuned pipes moan deep and raw -

Buddy slides his foot off the clutch
and the big coupe fishtails, screaming
through the sleepy streets
old folks in porch rockers, kids on bikes,
Bernie the barber, watering his daffodils,
everybody stops as shining green thunder
tears Sunday in two:

through the one blinking light
at the corner of Main and West Marlette,
one hand on the wheel,
one jamming the shifter for third,
he leaves football and American history,
pumping gas, and his father's drunkenness
blowing away in the exhaust.

We all watch: Doug and Randy and me wishing
him luck, wishing it was us.
Past the railroad tracks and grain elevators,
shrinking to a speeding blur,
a flash of light on the laundromat windows,
he looks gone.

But turning in a circle of dust and burning rubber
at Ruth's Café, the Willys pounds back,
drifts the curve, slides into the garage.
Buddy closes the door before the dust settles,
his engine crackling in cool down.

Esther Williams and a Friend Summering Off the Maine Coast

Two brown heads,
trail vees through the small slaps of waves,
move away from Town Beach to Job, the next island down.
They move unhurriedly as though they were leaving
a dinner party
at the home of some summer person,
swim as though they had the requisite two martinis,
a bit of melted butter staining a leg.

I run to the car for the binoculars,
a hand-held peek at lovers
who head for the quiet uninhabited
stands of cat spruce and bayberry on the far shore.

Sweet light molds their strokes, turns
their dancing to Monet on the water.
I thought young love,
or a pair of seals in a samba of elegance.

A slow turning of the focus knob
as they reach the steep stone of the next island.
Up from the salt they rise, brown garbed for the evening.
The rising moon plays silver on the buck's antlers
as he waits for his love to lead the way into the safety of the shadows.

Ridge Dancing

Early fall and we lug our tools -
hammers, saws, knives, and nails
from the beds of rusty trucks.
We pull yellow electric cords by the yard,
air hoses, blue chalk lines.

Fill our pouches with roofing nails.
Break the ladders out of frozen stacks.
We point them toward the sky and leave them
while we check and chat over a quick cup.
Shouldering shingles by the bundle, we climb.

Starting at the eaves, we snap lines
to keep our courses straight. Lay shingles
butt to butt, hurricane nail to
keep the weather out. Slap, tump-tump...

The trick is in the rhythm.

We could blaze away, fall down
spent before noon or set a pace
steady through the day. Tump-tump...

A smith once told me this:
One for the iron; one for the anvil.

An Asian master who spent a year
building one inlaid coffee table said:
A cut in the wood, a pass on the stone.
Always the rhythm.

The roofers' song begins like this:
Slap, tump-tump, tump- tump, tump- tump,
and again.
Our hammers drum
nail in hand, nail in roof.

On the ground they crank rock and roll.
Above, we have a rhythm of our own.
We climb, and sweat, muscles humming
slap-tump-tump;
faster than rain drops.

Flicker

On a silver wire
under a sky of mare's tails
unaware in this last moment
of me on the gravel road below
or of the arc of a small stone
thrown with no intent but
the humming of young muscle,
a flicker turned a bright eye
to his death then fell
into the oat-stubbled field -
a slight cloud of chaff.

Cupping his warmth in
my hands, I knew the final weight
of this small casting -
a pebble thrown without concern
that comes to rest like a mountain
in my heart
until my hands are still.

Toll Call

In the dark in nightmare I woke naked
holding the phone
standing twenty feet from my bed
A voice said, "Terry died tonight
under the full moon by the Mekong River."

Perhaps he had been remembering Michigan when the mortar hit,
a place he had touched and smelled and carried daily
a bit of earth molding in a folded Camel wrapper
kept in his pocket against the distance

Most of my life wars have raged
at a distance over there across the room
fleeting visions of choppers and body parts
the blooming of flame in someone else's night.

Rarely a threat to the safety of my room this house my family
bloodless and comfortable at the horizon of newscaster's lips
while I sat in this fishbowl deaf and untouched
worrying about the important things:

School work groceries my lover's birthday
I could start and stop the dying with a remote
for Christ's sake no blood on my carpet
able to hold my future son with my two good arms.

I refused to go to Nam so sensible
the right thing for me the only way I knew
to slow the bleeding
put out the flames . . .

But friends went and the sons of strangers
the daughter of the man beside me on the subway
Shari's boyfriend, Terry, the quiet guy
from the back row of chemistry.

Perhaps he had been remembering Michigan when the mortar hit
the long whine in my ear could have been the dial tone
of disconnect or the whistle of an incoming round
It has never left me that silence
the crazed screaming of shells the emptiness of a heart
no longer beating.

Before Coffee

Every morning the dark-robed crows
congregate in the pines at the edge of my yard,
sitting in small groups grumbling
until I step onto the lighted porch.

They grow quiet as monks,
cock their heads and mumble
perhaps in Latin
and we share an early prayer,
a *magnificat* for another day.

All winter we have met like this at dawn,
wind fluttering their black cassocks
as they peer down their noses
to view me at my lessons.

For a moment we inhale the crackling air
until they rattle with impatience, cackle
at my feeble attempts to see the face of God,
and the old men in the trees fly off.

Alchemy

November nights the moon
silvers rails into parallel
knives of light streaking away.
The low chuff of the coming 9:05
shakes the frost from the skeletal
heads of Queen Anne's lace,
steel wheels screech and clack
against the chill.
We stand shivering at the siding,
little ghosts in ground fog,
eyes fixed on the pennies,
awaiting transformation.

Falling into Lunacy

Every night standing at the bottom of the steep stairs,
I visited the little town in New Mexico where
Ansel Adams sold the moon a bill of goods.

He caught her in just the right turn as her robe fell open.
She would have left a town of women alone
husbands and sons walking blindly into the night
desert awash in her luminescence
until they found themselves
lost in the heat of a new day.
But she fell between their dreams
and their snores,
and lay soft in dirt floor corners.
In the new day's sweeping she was
indistinguishable from dust,
from fallen cobwebs.

Blessed Work

The conveyor clanks its chains,
pigeons explode, spiral up
the echoing tin.

I stand planted,
wild with balance.
grain rains from above.

Chunk-whick, slither and pitch,
my shovel fights the growing pile,
pulls from center out.

The shhhh of wheat fills the morning.
fills the air with dust-shattered light,
fills my eyes, fills the world

I shovel,
moving rain at the center
of an hourglass.

Chaff covered ghost,
god-boy of the barnyard,
arms swing and swing again.

Luminaria

I find them in the morning mud -
small pointed pools that hold skies
no larger than the hoof of a doe,
each a perfect mirror for a morning star.

With the coming light their curved edges melt,
the reflection flattening into a silver platter -
a whole day's brilliance spilling across the face of the cove,
lighting the edges of eel grasses,

limning the legs of green crabs
as they race for the shadows of stones,
for the deep wet seaweed that holds them cool
and close while the mirror slides away from the shore.

Sometimes in the dark, I hear the looking glass makers
moving like small winds from the edge of the woods,
the bucks snorting and chuffing their protection
as the does dance to some silent music

that must move between the stars and reeds
to draw them from their safety,
lead them into moonlight
bright enough to blur the difference

between their reflected eyes and the deep
fires of the night.

Resurrection

The night Bobby Inch died
my father came home wild-eyed and crying.
A cattle truck charging through the dusk
caught the paper boy high on its horns
threw him breathless to one side.

We wore the same shirt that day.
In flashing reds and blues, my father
saw the familiar shirt,
still against the blacktop.
felt me slipping from him.

Seeing Bobby's face,
some other father's son,
he raced home to rage and rant
and hold me, looking deep
into my wide open eyes.

Riding Shotgun, 1962

The old man pats the silver bulldog,
snaps the wipers free of ice and hoists me
to the shotgun seat of the '55 Mack.
In green from the dash light,
we log mileage, check provisions
coffee, doughnuts, Wrigley's spearmint gum.

Ghosts in white paper hats top our tank;
thump the door; give us thumbs up.
Three a.m. and a thousand gallons of grade B milk,
we slosh and roar
from the safety of Marlette lights.

Just the two of us
singing Danny Boy over diesel roar
riding high beam rails,
road rangers a world away from home,
a downshift apart,
my father's Camel winking one red eye
all the way to the smoking heart of Detroit.

Sitting close so we could hear,
we talk the night away.
He spilled stories of his childhood -
how alone he'd been in the city
but for the rented horse at Lincoln Park stables
who carried him away winter and summer
to find the place his father lived.

How his father played hockey for the Maple Leafs,
sold shoes for Sears in the off-season,
died of pneumonia in '29.

Back through small dark towns,
past barns rising from the fog.
Imlay City, then Burnside.
Shapes of tractors and balers
leaning toward the fences
or were they horses in the dark?
Slower now, close to home
and still secrets locked in blue ice -
my father's eyes.

Outside, the whicker of a quarter-horse at the edge
of a pasture, waiting like the china
palomino who grazed the bureau
between Dad's pocket watch
and his loose change.

Unexpectedly, a Love Poem

It was supposed to be about baseball,
about the change-up he saw coming
and the resultant stand-up triple.
It was supposed to be about trophies,
like the lost one, the last one, out in the shed.
It was supposed to be about Ree's supper:
Ree-potatoes, Ree-bread w/ real maple syrup,
deerheart and fiddlehead casserole,
about the four miles my brother
tracked that wounded leaking heart
through the wind chill and noisy crust,
about the men who stood around
the pickup bed, slapping my brother's back
congratulating and irritating him
with Michelob Light smelly smoke rings,
about the new George Strait CD
that carried the weary hunters home,
about the wives, wearier from years
of orange laundry and stories, who listen one
more time; this time one's a hunter's mother
and it was supposed to be about her pride.
It was never supposed to be a love poem.
It just was. They all are. If you give them time.

The Chevy Trucks Poem

I had a Nissan once
who lasted quite a while
but he wasn't much to look at
and he didn't do me any favors.

My younger years
found me a bit too attached
to a boy's Daddy's GMC
but he was only a Chevy wannabe.

And there may be only one Jeep
but I've had several
and they were all the same:
all performance, no comfort.

I test drove a few Dodges
but they were a bit *too* Dodge
different for me. Every time I
grab life by the horns, I get thrown.

Along the way, had a few
built Ford toughs
who were a tad *too* tough
and built to last — my ass.

No, nothing compares to the standby.
Got to find me a man in a Chevy truck:
strong, dependable, trustworthy.
He'll be there. Like a rock.

A Friend and Three Strangers

I am two and a half years old
with really pretty eyes
and pink barrettes
and my mother
just told a friend
and three strangers
that she dreams of
selling me, taking me
to the pawn shop
dropping me off
and my mother
laughs as she brags
that sometimes
she just locks me in a room
because I scream too much.
The strangers look at me with pity
as if I don't even know what I am
or what I am destined to become
and one of them whispers,
my mother did so many drugs
when she was pregnant,
it's no wonder I can't talk.
They think because I don't talk
I don't hear them call me dirty
and when I stare at them, they smile
and when I look away, they shake their heads
wondering if they should call someone
but they don't.
They just shake their heads.

Eternally Eighteen

I am afraid of the poem you might become, for in death
you are larger than life could ever be. Do I even have the right
to try to capture you, so big and brilliant in black and white,
framed between my parents on every wall I've ever known,
you are eternally eighteen. When asked who knows me best,
I think of a man I've never met. I think of knowing you well,
growing up knowing you right there, hearing your name every day,
wondering where you were and why they loved and missed you
so much, too little to understand loss or grief or life between.
I memorized the memories, stared at Little League portraits,
listened to your father strum and sing "I still miss someone"
on the guitar you bought him postmortem, he sang and cried.
I think of knowing you must have been as close to perfect,
as close to Christ, as any man could possibly be because
the greatest man I've ever known said that you were greater.
I think of knowing you well enough to know they are right
as they drone on and on that my brother is your spitting image.
I too have spent hours staring at your face black and white,
framed between my parents on every wall I've ever known,
you are eternally eighteen. How old are you in heaven? What
might you look like as an angel of the highest sort, breathing
faith into all those you left behind, smiling gently at your own face
bookmarking some appropriate passage in every family Bible,
sighing softly every March when your parents decorate the altar
with your yellow roses you never knew you loved as much
as they now claim you do? And in the paper that birthday that same
seraphic face, same black and white as the face black and white,
framed between my parents on every wall I've ever known,
you are eternally eighteen. Do you still sing the same songs that
you sang as a young man? Because I know them all by heart and I
would find comfort in knowing that when I sing, you are singing along.

Language

~ for Alex

If you're gonna understand, let me explain:
Around these here parts, people communicate
with truck horns. Depending on duration
and frequency, a sequence of honks can say:

- Haven't seen you in a while.
- Excited now to see you.
- Goin' to town, be right back.
- Goin' by your house now, thought you'd like to know.
- My father honks to you so I do too.
- Fuck you.
- Fuck you too.

The most versatile language, with minimal effort
we honk our way through these small towns
never thinking anything of it. So now with that
background information, you'll understand my surprise
when my friend asked me why I was honking
to the cemetery on the Kingfield Road
long, loud, laboriously, with rhythm
and who the hell I was honking to
and now you'll understand how much sense
it made to both of us when I said,
I was just sayin' hi to my dad.

Thieves

They came
in the night
softly
on fresh snow
leaving tracks
no one willing
to follow.

They crawled
around inside
of me, touching
everything
leaving fingerprints
no one willing
to recognize.

They picked
through my treasures
taking only
what suited them
leaving the rest
of my life
in a pile
on the floor.
I'm not yet willing
to be grateful.

Out Here

I know why he killed himself.
You know, the old man
who spent thirty years
trying to break out of prison
and his last two
aching to get back in.
I know him, how he missed
that cold comfort of gray.
I too, have seen colors be scary.
I know why he carved his name
in the headboard at the boarding house,
before he swallowed the stolen pills.
For thirty years they barked his name.
He hasn't heard it since. After living
the same day over and over,
regimen and routine,
now he wakes without schedule.
There are no friends here.
There is no family.
He left all of that behind.
Though he didn't know it then,
prison gave him purpose.
It's lonely out here.

Thousand Dollar Thumbs

You cut the left one off with a tablesaw.
Good doctor sewed it back on. Called you lucky.
Next summer, the right one got gobbled up
by a bear trap. Took twenty stitches to repair it.
Driving home, your father coined the pair:
your thousand dollar thumbs. I didn't know
these stories the first time I felt them,
left one bigger than it should be and crooked.
right one shrunken and hard as a knot,
scarred up like maps my fingers followed.
Ugly and perfect, your thumbs traced out my spine.
Callous caress so extraordinary, call me lucky.
Now our grandkids hang off them, unaware of their history.
Now morning's clumsy thumbs fumble shirt buttons.
But I am here to help you. Call us both lucky.

Final Draft

(for Minnie E. Bowden 1915-2000)

Where will they find my last poem?

On the hard drive
or on a Burger King napkin?

I hope it's a bookmark for some Psalm
not a soggy coaster for some longneck.

I really hope they find it
before it goes through the wash.

There's no way to know
where they'll find my last poem

but when they do
please tell them to

bury it with me.
I'm not finished yet.

Johnny Cash Died Today

And they played *Hurt* every other song on
    every station.
And in Southern Maine a Vietnam veteran
    opened a reserved bottle of scotch.
And on a street in Montreal
    a prostitute pulled her small coat
    a little tighter around her heart.
And in New York, a man on death row
    cried for the first and last time.
And in a California penitentiary
    general population had an undeclared
    moment of silence.
And a mute woman in a mental institution
    began to hum *I Walk the Line*.
And a carpenter in Kansas
    stopped his hammer mid-swing
    and looked at the sky.
And somewhere in Detroit
    a newborn baby began to cry.

and He'll plant his beautiful feet
upon this mountain
and the dead of all the ages
who believed on Him will rise
and I'll be one in the first resurrection
when He comes   when He comes
    when He comes

And somewhere in Arizona
      a little Native American girl with
      red velvet ribbons looped over pigtails
      danced and sang *Ring of Fire*
      for her grandparents.
And a preacher in Massachusetts
      wondered for the first time if
      he'd been wrong to condemn
      country music.
And a man in a bar in Kentucky
      put down his last drink and left.
And every artist in Nashville
      wrote a song.
And a young boy in New Jersey
      asked his father,
      "Who's Johnny Cash?"
      and his father told him.
And the weeping willow cried.
And Waylon Jennings smiled.
And Jack Cash laughed.
And June Carter spread her arms wide.
And so did Jesus Christ.
And heaven shook
      boom batta
          boom batta   boom batta
                                            boom batta
   boom batta
        boom
          boom
            boom.
And a humble star
Dressed in black
Nodded his head
And said,
"Hello. I'm Johnny Cash."

I always turn the radio

off
when I stop at the
stop
sign
by the white cross
where you died

I always turn the radio
off
some sort of ceremonial
moment of silence

today
I forgot
for the first time
to turn the radio
off

I was talking
to a new friend

can you forgive me
for forgetting
to turn the radio
off
and also
for living

My Dead Daughter

Every spring
my dead daughter spraypaints
PLEASE DON'T DRINK AND DRIVE
on the road where she died.

My dead daughter has a flute
at the grammar school
for kids whose parents can't afford
a flute of their own.

My dead daughter
sends fifth graders
to art camp
every year.

This year
instead of marching with them
my dead daughter is helping
send her classmates to college.

My dead daughter's
changing the world.

To Do

You narrowed your
forty-five-dollars-an-hour-eyes
and asked who
I was trying to please.
Who exactly, I so badly
needed to keep happy.
So I told you and you let out
a well-trained, "She's DEAD!"
I, stunned, knew that,
failed to see your point.
She's dead, yes, but still . . .
There's the grave to rake
to weed, to decorate.
Flowers to change, photos to rearrange.
And so many cards to mail!
Mother's Days just keep coming,
birthdays, significant dates that if I forget,
will be forgotten. There are people
to love, people to remember. Little
brothers are graduating high school.
People are getting married. Babies born,
nieces baptized, nephews christened.
Life keeps on happening.
So *no*, I tell you
ten years past your leather couch.
She's *not* dead.
There's still too much to do.

Jail Workshop:
Things I Can't Say

I asked each inmate
to create a list titled:
Things I Can't Say.

And the man in the corner wrote:
I want to cut you, fuck you,
bleed you, kill you motherfucker.

And the woman beside me wrote:
To my son, I love you.

And the man beside her:
To my friend who hung himself,
you are weak and I hate you
and I forgive you.

And the blue-eyed boy with long hair:
I think I'm Jesus.

And the quiet man:
I'd like to tell the system
it's not working.

And the man
supposed to be the baddest:
I was wrong.

dining in

seventy nine years —
        won't go out to a restaurant
— old

stubborn and stuck —
        just no need of it
— in his ways

married for sixty —
        never took his wife out to eat
— years

hundreds of thousands of —
        living in a trailer
— dollars tucked away

miserable miser doesn't mind if —
        restaurants are dirty
— his old wife complains

he'll die without trying —
        who knows who cooks that food
— a quarterpounder or a filet mignon

and his wife —
        when he's not looking
— just started going on her own

New Year's Day

You never start completely new.
All you think and do
wakes up with you in the morning.
Old habits stay.
Remember the first day at school?
The notebooks fresh, no classes missed.
And then it doesn't work out right.
The papers wait until too late.
The textbooks wait and then are never read.
And love is just the same.
Even when it starts out fine
you say some things you shouldn't say
and see your lover hurt and distance stays.
And what you write is not what you want to write.
What you want to write is precise and moving,
but what you write is sloppy and dull.
You never start completely new.
Like a yawn or the need for coffee,
or the way you clear your throat before speaking,
old habits stay.
At best you fit a little in each day,
acceptance of yourself and lover,
one answer right from pages of doodles.

For Roger Who Died at Work

How I expect him to come in
refreshed and more focused than
he ever was, immediately begin,
"Let me tell you what happened to me."
And the meeting would leave us all
with a sense of calm about the future,
like cave-dwellers observing the sun's
return in winter, how that extra hour
must have felt, to gather wood or hunt meat.
This is what Roger would talk about,
the coming of the light. How I expect him
to have the paperwork complete, on time
and magical, with a list of things-to-do
that is exactly right, exactly true,
identifying needs that you and I
ignore or despair of ever touching,
and an action plan that is exactly right,
exactly true, as simple as turning
to face the person beside you,
as simple as knowing that one day
the wind will carry your name,
and on that day, late in winter,
you too will leave the office
and not come back.

Tantramar

We have years now and memory as common
as weeds in a field. Milkweed and goldenrod.
Black-eyed Susan and Queen Anne's lace.
And you have taught me there is worth in every plant
and stopped me from calling the bush hog guy
and cutting them all down to grass. And had
me ease the yellow rosebush behind
the globe thistle and pick white aster for the table.
We have years now and the names of places,
Albany, Nashua, San Francisco, Monemvasia.
Our map to tend, postcards spilling out of drawers
and mixing with Legos.

One year in Canada, on the museum map
in St. John, we saw how the French built a fort
and the British burned it down and the British
built a fort and the French burned it down.
On the border of New Brunswick
and Nova Scotia, beside a cold marsh,
was a fort named Tantramar. We walked the walls
and sighted along the cannons, thought of war
bringing men to the grave in spurts and prayed
not to see it happen.

The motel was Tantramar as well. After supper
we settled in. You read your book, back against
the pillows. I flipped channels, watched a ball game.
We drank two Molsons from the cooler and then
we touched each other, entered in the ancient dance.
And you became a wind that grows in strength
in the night, so that I was like a man who hears
a storm against the house, goes to the door
and opens it and finds it nearly pulled off the hinges,
the trees swaying violently and limbs down in the yard.
We entered that wind and I am grateful.

In the morning we walked in a garden beside the fort
and talked about a child who did not come until later,
but who was banging and kicking when he did come,
as wild as the squash plant that runs out of the garden
headed for the picnic table. Soon he will be ready
to load and fire, load and fire. We give him plants
instead, teach him how to dig the earth, pray
this is what he will choose. We have years now.
I learn the names of the plants for you.

Light My Fire

The night I saw the Doors
on the Ed Sullivan Show
in Mike Testa's living room
the face of Jim Morrison
with his long Jesus curls
and the phallic microphone up to his mouth
filled the black and white TV screen
as he sang snakelike,
"Come on, baby, light my fire."
Mike's old man said something obligatory
about "the long-haired faggot,"
but Mike's two teenaged sisters
were kindled in a way I had never seen.
They leaned forward on the couch,
their eyes fixed, their backs arched,
"like freakin' zombies," we would have said,
but Mike was bored and wanted
to go back to his room and play
the Monkees forty-five, "Daydream Believer,"
on his record player. And although
I saw them drooling and saw
the skinny breasts that hung down
inside of Jennie's shirt as well,
I was Aladdin outside the cave
with no magic words and only
the vaguest idea of the treasure within.
And it was a long time after
sixth grade and Bradford, Pennsylvania,
before I would learn how to share
that incredible fire.

Fear

Tonight I walk alone
In the dark and the cold
Through the woods behind the house,
And in the dark I am afraid.
The apple trees are black and twisted,
Resembling men gone insane.
They stand in shadows and wave their arms
In anger and I think of how a real man
Could rush out from behind with a knife
And not be seen until too late.
I think of how on Channel 6
They told of police searching for Leon Michaud
While his pickup truck sat alone
In the parking lot of Shop'N Save.
They found him dead and dumped beside the road.
I do not want my car to sit alone.

Tonight in the dark and the cold
I reach the dirt road, turn a corner
And find a mound that looks exactly like a grave,
And I think of a door being closed
And myself alone forever,
Until, a few steps later I find it's
A pile of beer cans buried in the snow.
Because I know that someday
I will find my own grave
Tonight I am afraid to walk alone
Along the gas line to the top of the hill,
And yet, because I do, I hear the brook
Make noise louder than a machine,
And see the lights of a jet trail red
And move in a line across the sky
As steady as memory, as bright as any
Of a billion stars.

Opening Day

The snow had pulled back to the woods
and the sun was as bright as a new uniform.
We rode our bikes to the high school.
The big boys were ready, not for the British
at Lexington and Concord, but for Wells.
We held them scoreless in the first.

I was amazed to see Joseph Bragdon
playing first base. The older brother of
my brother's friend, I'd seen him blubbering
when his mother told him about the diet
she was putting him on and then seen him
stuffing Funny Bones into his mouth at Bracy's
half an hour later. He taught us words, tits
and cock, and offered to show us pictures
in dirty magazines.

We stayed away from Fat Joe and I
couldn't believe the coach didn't see
what kind of person he was. But in the
bottom of the first, one on and two out,
Joseph Bragdon got a hold of a pitch
and drove it all the way to the pine trees
at the edge of Stilphen's field.

I still remember the crack of the bat
as loud as a gunshot in the neighbor's yard.
When the ball cleared the left fielder's head
it looked like a great migratory bird
on its way to Canada. It soared over
the cut grass of the ballfield, over the tall grass
beyond the field, all the way to the pine needles.

I thought the umpire would stop the game
right there and we would all try and figure out
how Joseph Bragdon could hit a baseball so far
and Fat Joe just stood there watching it as well.

But their left fielder wasn't as easily impressed.
He took off like a good soldier in a battle charge
at Gettysburg. He found the ball and threw to
the center fielder set up ten yards deep in the tall grass
who threw to the shortstop in the middle of left field
who threw to second base as if they'd practiced
that very play. Fat Joe lumbered in just ahead
of the throw.

The score was one to nothing.

I don't remember much else about the game,
except I don't suppose Joe scored from second
too many times on a single, and Wells beat us
something like 11-5. In the box score it wouldn't
have looked like enough and I seemed to be
the only one bothered by the enormity of it,
although I did hear one old guy say,
"That one the Bragdon boy hit..."

But I learned then you don't have to be
a good guy to hit a baseball half a mile
and the world just keeps going on,
inning after inning.

Beverly

The witches in *Macbeth* were prettier than Beverly.
She had hair on her chin and bad teeth she didn't like to brush.
But she didn't scream or fight or act like her roommate, Linda,
who screamed all the time and grabbed things out of people's hands,
saying, "That's MY radio! That's MY book!"
So we all liked Beverly. She asked a lot of questions though.
"Hey, Dave, can we have pork chops? Huh, can we have pork chops?"

Every night of spaghetti, meat loaf or chicken
she sat at the table quietly, but when we had pork chops
it was, "Oh boy, I like pork chops!"
She ate them quickly and brought her plate to the kitchen
and did her chore without having to be told.

"Why do my eyes go up? They go up and I can't
make them go down. Why do my eyes go up?"
"If I get upset I don't have to go back to O.D. Heck, do I?
This is my home, isn't it?"

"What's heaven like? You know, where you go when you die?
Huh, what's heaven like?"

She would ask those questions in the van on the way
to the workshop or in the living room with everyone
watching TV. I thought I was being helpful when I told her,
"Beverly, heaven is a nice home where you can stay
no matter what and you can have pork chops every night."

Although I worked in the house for barely a year
I still can see her in the front yard in a lawn chair
looking up at the sun. I do not know what
they tell her now or what she has for supper.

She never trusted my answer anyway, so kept asking,
"Hey, Dave, what's heaven like? You know, where
you go when you die? Can you have pork chops there really?
Huh, can we have pork chops? Can we have pork chops?"

Salt to the Brain

(In Praise of Poets)

As a rule we are not the brain surgeons
or the bridge builders. We did not figure
how to make water flow in a pipe
or keep airplanes stable in flight.
Instead, we stood in a circle and chanted,
"All praise to the most beautiful bridge,"
then walked across it.

As a rule we do not meet the payroll
or keep the factories open.
Others figured how enzymes work
and built hydraulic brakes.
Instead, we were the ones at the machines
whose idea it was to sing, "Happy Birthday,"
or "Nobody Knows the Trouble I've Seen."

In this world the moneychangers change money.
The nurses nurse and the lawyers lawyer.
My mother feeds the stray cats that come
to the screen door of her house in Marion Oaks.
The orange tiger has a nasty scratch.
The poets take note,
add this small pinch of salt to the brain,
our gift to the taste of existence.

A History of Wanting

It was a hard day for the infielders.
The fortieth hot day in a row,
the field baked hard as a sidewalk,
both starters throwing breaking balls down,
the ground balls came like punches,
dig and throw, dig and throw,
like a farmer in a rocky field,
the crops harvested before winter,
the runners beaten by just a step.
The shortstop handles seven chances
flawlessly, two double plays, when
in the seventh he dives into the hole
to stop a two hop bullet, sets and throws
and the ball soars over the first baseman's head.
Two runs score on the play
and the hometown fans jeer
as their pennant hopes
fade away.

There have always been more ways to lose than win.
Remember Dalton Jones? Gary Allenson?
Wim Remmerswal? Jeff Sellers? Sam Horn?
Young men with grace and power,
but the pitchers couldn't quite keep the ball
off the bat or the hitters hit a curveball.
And the guys who could play didn't when they had to.
Yaz in seventy-eight, popping the first pitch
to Nettles at third base. And how many times
do we have to hear about that stray dog of a ground ball
rolling through Buckner's legs in eighty-six?
Come on, the guy was a fielder, playing
with a bad back and now his wife can't go in
the grocery store without being harassed.
In high school on the couch with Linda and her father,
talking too much, but they had to know about Lonborg's
knee and Bill Rohr's one hitter. Yaz was playing first
that night and hitting everything on the nose. In the sixth
he was pulled off the bag by a bad throw and he spun

like a toreador and slapped the runner on the shoulder
and we started, for it was beautiful, and unexpected,
like a deer flushed in the woods or kissing Linda on
the mouth after her old man went to bed.

In seventy-nine Evans juiced a ball
into the great empty ocean of right center
and the Chicken Man, Micky Rivers, who looked
like one of those wooden men you bounce on your knee
when he walked, but was an antelope when he ran,
became a flying bird man with his glove reaching,
impossibly, the spot where the ball arrives,
and he slides with the ball intact and though
he rises and squawks and throws a relay
that actually rolls to second base the rally
is damaged and then Hobson strikes out.

I could go on like this for a long time
for I've had the ballgame on my whole life
and when I've been away in the morning
I've gone looking for the box score
and found the players' names lined up
and their hits and runs recorded.

In October, sixty-seven, when our lessons were done,
my sixth grade teacher turned on the seventh game
of the World Series and the score flashed 7-1 St. Louis
and my stomach knotted so I couldn't drink my carton of milk.
My aunt, who does not care about baseball,
but cried just the same the day the picture of Tony
Conigliaro, his eye swollen big as a baseball
and black as a frying pan appeared on the front page
of the Record American, now declares, "When
the Red Sox win the World Series we will lose
a great knowledge of wanting."
But already I see the fastball thrown belt high
to Ortiz with the bases loaded and think,
this year, this year.

Borrowed Time

I will not die tonight.
I will lie in bed with
my wife beside me,
curled on the right
like an animal burrowing.
I will fit myself against her
and we will keep each other warm.

I will not die tonight.
My son who is seven
will not slide beneath the ice
like the boy on the news.
The divers will not have to look
for him in the cold water.
He will call, "Daddy, can I get up now?"
in the morning.

I will not die tonight.
I will balance the checkbook,
wash up the dishes
and sit in front of the TV
drinking one beer.

For the moment I hold a winning ticket.
It's my turn to buy cold cuts
at the grocery store.
I fill my basket carefully.

For like the rain that comes now
to the roof and slides down the gutter
I am headed to the earth.
And like the others, all the lost
and all the lovers, I will follow
an old path not marked on any map.

Cultivating Joy

My new life begins this moment.
I am ready for it now.
I've been learning a new skill,
the ability to see magic everywhere.
Like Miss Rita on Romper Room,
she held up her mirror, looked through
the television and said, "I see David,
I see Leslie, I see their children, Sam
and Mira." I see the spruce tree beside the
driveway and the Chevy Nova parked
under it. The lunches are on the counter.
My new life begins this moment.
It has happened before, buying gas
on Center Street, returning a phone call
on the answering machine, yet
I never saw it, or saw the process
going on around me, that death
will be like jumping into deep water.
That summer of swimming lessons
they rowed us to the raft,
Mrs. Wormwood in the water
reached up and took my hand
and I fell into a great airless womb.
When my body rose, broke the surface
and breathed, my life was changed forever.
I, too, was a spirit. I could change
so easily from air to water
and back to air. We swam to the shore.
They followed in the rowboat.
My new life begins this moment.
All the time it was there, yet like
Dorothy in *The Wizard of Oz*,
I had to learn it for myself,
that someday I will go home
and will need no ruby slippers.
My new life begins this moment.

My Television Does Not Listen to Me

My television does not listen to me.
It talks on and on, like a selfish lover,
not really concerned with my needs.
It wants and wants and wants
me to buy a new car, a new phone,
beer, Pepsi and jeans. I tell it
I do not need a stronger medicine
for my headache, I need to know
why I am sick.

My television does not listen to me,
even though I try to tell it how my
father drove the station wagon to Pepe's
farm in Vermont and it snowed all day.
The last five miles we flew through
the dark on the unplowed road
and got stuck at the bottom of the hill.
They wrapped us in blankets and brought us
to Meme's kitchen on the back
of a tractor.

My television does not listen to anyone,
when all around I hear material
for so many good shows. The cashier
at Shop'N Save tells her friend,
"He hasn't asked, but I'll say yes
if he does," and my son in first grade
adds, " I dreamed I was being chased
and you were there but not really."
I hear the birds and the squirrels
call and chatter, call and chatter
all day long in the back yard
and the cat with the one white paw
screams out during the late show.

We could talk about this,
we could talk about all of this,
if my television would only listen.

Writing Poetry

There are always so many words you can use
and so many ways you can fit them together.
But like a Rubik's cube the more you turn
the more you lose the color you want.
Each direction becomes not quite right
or something else altogether.

And there are so many things to say.
At any given moment all you need
is what you have in your pocket.
But when you add this moment
and that moment, pretty quickly,
you end up not with a shed,
or even a barn full of stuff, but
a universe crowded with memory
and thought. How can we ever
pull out pages clean and sharp?

Yes, there are rules.
Tell the truth. Although you can make it up.
Get to the point. But don't rush.
Accept that your effort will be insignificant,
but remind yourself how important it is
that you do it.

Despite your striving for lupine,
the words will always be ragweed.
But the fields will be brilliant.

Postcard from Mexico

After a week of rain, your card arrived,
but not the sun. I read it still soaked;
some of the writing bled. Here, towels and jeans
never quite dry, and sooty water swells the gutters.

Caught in the cold rain, the city is helpless;
drowned worms thread the sidewalks.
All night, cars hiss; I dream of you,
brown on white sand.

Out walking, feet wet, I pause
in the scent rising from a laundromat.
Where you are, white walls hold the long day's heat
and careless flowers leaven the night air.

The Wreath People

I'm sick of them,
these wreaths -
brown, dessicated,
with forlorn red bows
they linger on doors and windows
in the strengthening sun.
There must be fifty in my neighborhood alone.
It's almost Easter.
They have to go.
Green and fresh, in dark December
they gladdened the heart
but it's long past time to
recycle, bury or burn.
I fantasize about roaming the streets
picking off wreaths with
silent rubber bullets.
I should get a medal from the mayor.
The Wreath People puzzle me -
they live among us, but why?
Is it laziness, inertia, an arcane ritual,
or do the dead wreaths
mark their houses for the mother ship?

Casco Bay, July

There are many watershed moments,
not Hallmark, not Kodak
I will remember about knowing you,
and wish I could purge from memory.
But the evening we paddled
out from Mackworth Island
on the limpid, calm bay
in a slight, freshening breeze
and twelve curious seals slid off their grey rock
and encircled us in the water
while we sat motionless, scarcely breathing,
kayaks barely moving in the still water
and the only sound was the crying of gulls . . .
the seals' whiskery faces and dark eyes
regarding us solemnly
while they kept us in their circle,
diving and resurfacing and moving
around us so gracefully -
that moment
I do not wish away.

On the Dog Planet

it doesn't matter
how funny-looking you are

or that your ancestors
did not arrive
on the Mayflower

or even that you are
missing a limb

the world of the senses
is never dull

food is always delicious
and no one is ever
anorexic

bad hair days
don't faze your friends

tempers may flare a bit
but hardly anyone
wants to fight

love is everlasting

and every citizen
has a big heart

Poetry Reading of My Dreams

All the poets are beautiful,
The young men wear those endearingly
    baggy pants
and Irish sweaters

but you can still sense how buff they are.
They have soulful eyes
    soft voices
and they read their gorgeous poems
    perfectly.

Every one of them looks into my eyes
    at the last line.

I'm in the back row, looking fabulous
    and flush with the success of
    my latest book of poems.

The women poets are lovely, too,
    and when it's over they vie
    to congratulate me and press
    their soft faces to mine.

I listen and drink in the poems
    while I make my choice
    of new protégé, lover, muse.

Revenge of the Metaphors

Untrue lover,
your treachery laid me low.
When the ugly end came
I carried a big empty space
just behind my breastbone
for a year
and twenty years
haven't revised the memory.
You were the soft slipper
hiding a scorpion,
a familiar knife
that slips and draws blood,
the safe dropped
on the unwary pedestrian.

Artifice

Confession: when the fire alarm went off in the hotel
I grabbed my wallet and laptop
and pulled my raincoat on over my nightgown
but I also hastily combed my hair
and swiped on some lipstick.
I'm the woman at the all-female retreat
who puts on mascara for a hike in the woods.
It's not that I can't stand my naked face
but presentation counts, and old habits persist.
Maybe it's my Southern roots
though by Southern girly standards
I'm underdressed, un-made up,
certainly insufficiently bejeweled
and accessorized.
I admire how vanity falls away
from some wise, aging women
but I don't see it happening to me.
When I'm ninety I'll still flirt
with cabdrivers and my doctor,
and be the wily rebel
who smuggles a robe
into the nudist resort.

Feng Shui

"It's good to have poems that begin with tea and end with God."

~ *Robert Bly*

Cleaning out the pantry,
I come across an old straw box
filled with a motley assortment
of tea bags
going back years,
and stand there musing
over their histories,
their provenance.

This Ceylon tea from a former friend
who faded away when I got a divorce;
this jasmine tea a souvenir from an ex
lover's trip to Japan - the one
where I called his hotel at 3 AM
and a woman answered;
this herbal raspberry tea from a
sensible vegetarian friend,
during my regrettable phase
of swearing off caffeine and sugar.

These tiny scented envelopes
recall my younger selves
and those formerly vivid people
once close enough to drink tea with,
to give and take small gifts.
All the ghostly tea-drinkers
are lost to me - gone
to other countries,
other friends,
unknown lovers,
gone to seed,
gone to California,
gone to God.

After the Poetry Reading
(Moon Poem # 5,753)

The poets, blooming with beards and vivid hair,
stride away, minds crowded with images,
new metaphors spilling out with the lamplight
into the chilly street,
discarded similes
crunched under their boots on the snow.

The ones not writing in their heads
compose sound,
the babble of poetic gossip,
envy, competition.
Above them all, unnoticed, floats
the patient, much-described moon,
writing a watery line
across the night sky.

thunderstorm at spirit lake

leaves flew
the tent flapped
like an inhabited kite
that would rise
and wheel over the lake
you danced
wet naked and cursing
around the tent
trying to fasten the rain fly
in the lightning's glare
I saw you
and the moving trees
rain sheeted down
while our laughter
soared above the lake
and split
the lighted sky

The Perfect Day

You wake with
no aches
in the arms
of your beloved
to the smell of fresh coffee
you eat a giant breakfast
with no thought
of carbs
there is time to read
with a purring cat on your lap
later you walk by the ocean
with your dog
on this cut crystal day
your favorite music and the sun
fill the house
a short delicious nap
under a fleece throw
comes later
and the phone doesn't ring
at dusk you roast a chicken,
bake bread, make an exquisite
chocolate cake
for some friends
you've been missing
someone brings you an
unexpected present
and the wine is just right with the food
after a wonderful party
you sink into sleep
in a clean nightgown
in fresh sheets
your sweetheart doesn't snore
and in your dreams
an old piece of sadness
lifts away

Emergency Instructions

To panic is expected.
You may practice: sleep alone,
read his letters over and over,
renew your library card.
Acquire a pet.
You will need supplies:
light bulbs, Kleenex, whiskey.
Nights will be hardest.
Stay off the telephone; draw the curtains.
You will not be contacted again.

Stealing Lilacs

A guaranteed miracle,
it happens for two weeks each May,
this bounty of riches
where McMansion, trailer,
the humblest driveway
burst with color - pale lavender,
purple, darker plum -
and glorious scent.
This morning a battered station wagon
drew up on my street
and a very fat woman got out
and starting tearing branches
from my neighbor's tall old lilac -
grabbing, snapping stems, heaving
armloads of purple sprays
into her beater.
A tangle of kids' arms and legs
writhed in the car.
I almost opened the screen door
to say something,
but couldn't begrudge her theft,
or the impulse
to steal such beauty.
Just this once,
there is enough for everyone.

Mud Season

After a brutal Maine winter
the world dissolves
in weak sunshine and water.
Mud sucks at your shoes.
It's impossible to keep the floors
or the dogs clean.
Peeling layers of clothes like onion skins,
you emerge pale, root-like, a little dazed
by brighter light.
You haven't looked at your legs
in months
and discover an alarming new geography
of veins and flaws.
Last year you scoffed at people
who got spray-tanned
but it's starting to appeal.
Your only consolation is the company of others
who haven't been to Nevis
or Boca Raton,
a pale army
of fellow radishes,
round onions,
long-underground tubers.

Letter Perfect

~ *for Dennis Camire*

let us praise O
so round, friendly,
the circle with no opening
a letter of distinction:
Ovid, Odysseus, Ozymandias
of odd instruments,
oboe and ocarina
traveler to exotic places - the
Orient, Odessa, Opalocka, Oz.
Imagine the peculiar all-O diet:
okra, olives, oatmeal, Oreos, oranges,
osso buco, or oolong tea !
The natural world would greatly miss O -
that ocelot in the oleander,
the owl perched in an oak
and the osprey winging over the orchard,
where an opossum feigns sleep.
Some O names make us laugh -
Ophelia Butt, Olive Oyl, Paddy O'Furniture,
Oprah as Orca
and think of the great Oscars -
Wilde, Levant, Peterson, Meyer, and
the sleek golden Hollywood prize.
Where would sexy writing be without
Oral, orgasm, onyx and opal, the story of O ?
O, most perfect letter,
you contain so much that is important -
and best of all, you are always
in love.

To My Cat with an Eating Disorder

You were thrown out of a moving vehicle
on a dirt road
in chilly winter downeast Maine,
little fur scrap, and I hope you don't
carry that memory with you,
but the hunger, the deep fear
that you'll never see food again
is still there five years later
when you are huge and sleek,
a sumo Buddha of a cat.

I've seen you, after a big meal,
heave yourself from a sound sleep,
pad into the kitchen, launch your bulk
onto the counter, and check the food supply,
then crouch there chewing and chewing,
green eyes empty, concentrating
on your burden, your compulsion,
doggedly eating, whether you want to or not.

There are stories about Holocaust or
Depression survivors whose refrigerators
and pantries are always full, just in case,
how some of them still wake in the night
and check their abundant supplies,
run their hands over the packages,
or eat without hunger, just because they can.

Cat, I stand in the dark kitchen
stroking your broad back,
wishing I could banish the fears
of one small, common creature,
those bad dreams that awaken you,
that hollow place in your memory
which can never be filled.

Ways of Looking

(1)
I inch my left foot slowly forward,
knowing that somewhere under the gray hay whitened
with pigeon droppings must be the trap door.
I lift the matted hay with the toe of my shoe
until cracked boards appear.

I kneel in the dust and mark with my forefinger
the rectangle of entrance, then lift with both hands
until the trap door's rusted hinges drop off
and rattle down wooden steps
to the concrete below. Taste of gray dust rises
in a cloud that I brush away with a sweep
of my head. The boards of the door fall apart
like my past. I worry that under my feet
the floor, too, might give way.

(2)
So I lean cautiously over the hole, as if
it were more than an entrance to the main floor
of the barn, as if something more important
than hay bales had slid down, catching briefly
on the jagged edge of a board, landing roughly
but muted, a soft thud, on the cement floor.
I notice that the stairway hangs almost loose,
nails pulling out, and that my foot on the top step
would send it crashing, permanently,
after the hay bales of my memory.
I carefully back away.

(3)
I see even less of the main floor from the large
sliding door at the end of the barn,
my face against the crack where one half
meets the other, where the sun lights a dagger-
thin strip from ceiling to floor.
I squint, looking for stanchions,
for pens filled with calves. As hard as I push,
I cannot budge the metal wheels
frozen in their track. When I kick, the door
bounces back, reverberates, then grows still,
leaving only the dagger of light
by which to see.

Gathering Immortality

Gathering eggs I discovered early to be
something between art and war, sliding
my hand slowly under the chicken

where the egg might be, if she
had carried out her proper function.
It was always guesswork, feeling

among the bristling feathers
and the softly scratching straw
for the brittle touch of the shell

hidden in the wooden box open
to the front and high enough to keep
the possums out. The hen would strike

with a short downward motion,
pull back and strike again, thinking,
perhaps, of future generations lost

After Haying

I lie down to rest
under the hay wagon, the short remnants
of hay bristling and prickling,
bristling and prickling my hands,
and my back through
a sweat-soaked T-shirt,
lying still in my great tiredness
under the wooden slats hiding from sun,
thanking God for work done.

Too Much Bull

There's an old ring in the elm bark
in the tree behind our house, rusted,
almost overgrown, formerly attached
by chain to a ring in a bull's nose,
a country link in the Great Chain
of Being philosophers talked much about.

Once my father was cornered by a bull
in the barnyard—no laughing matter.
My brother rescued him with a pitchfork
before the bull, mad as hell over something,
could slam my father through the fence.

Another bull, having smashed through
the gate of his pen, chased a man I know up
and down the long driveway of a barn,
man and bull sliding and slipping on wet
concrete. The man escaped, but it took
himself and three neighbors to get that bull
back where he belonged.

Going modern with artificial insemination,
my father decided to get rid of our
final bull just before I left for college.
The old bull wasn't getting the job done
anymore, either not caring about the task
at hand or unable to handle the challenge.
I never missed him.

Years later, driving back roads by pastures
green with rich, autumn grass, I spied
a big bull, fat and lazy, pushing his head up
against a tree. An apple or two fell down,
and I had a momentary flashback to childhood,
boy racing, bull pursuing, a gnarled apple tree,
and taking those tree limbs easily, like
a ladder, almost to the top. The bull looked up,
shook his short horns, snorted once or twice,
and eyed me as if I were a big, juicy apple.

I drove on, red as an apple, young as a child,
hearing a limb creak, but not seeing a bull
anywhere, and feeling happy about it.

Childhood Past

Burying my dog was easier than plowing
a field, harder than planting an Easter bulb
for spring blooming. We expected no great crop
from this digging, this planting the seed
of childhood, barks frozen in the slightly open mouth,
the feet that ran to call now slower than molasses,
warm petting-flesh flat and hard, life to leather.

I dreamed, though, there might be some bloom,
yellow or purple, leaning its fragile head into sun,
a thin stalk green-leaved, touch of perfume.
I watched, instead, the summer come and go, winter
fall white and cold, other seasons, an eternity
or two: and the hard silence unbearable at times,
a hand aching to be licked, fingers stroking air.

Transplanting

You can't transplant a dogwood
I was told. The roots are too long,
the tree's life too fragile,

but we tried: spading the earth
gently as if to strike hard would
make its roots bleed, stooping

like parents over the tree
torn from its bed, wrapping
the exposed roots in newspapers,

setting it all in a large garbage bag
which we watered as if all
that poets and philosophers have said

of water's life-giving spirit
were more than feeble symbol
to fill in acres of belief.

Then we carried it back in our van
from the Midwest to the East,
even when the boy pumping gas

gawked at it and made some joke
about portable shade. When I turned into
my drive, I knew it was as good as dead.

Hands Reaching

A young boy, I was primed
for climbing, eyeing the oats bin
and its top, a crosshatching of boards
flaked with end-of-year fragments
left over from the top's
double duty as a hayloft.

I climbed and climbed, up the wooden
ladder, foot reaching gingerly for
the next step, hands gripping and
pulling, even a young boy's weight heavy.
I made it and exulted, exulted

all too soon. There came a time
when getting down was even more vital
than climbing up. But that distance
multiplied looking down, and neither hands
nor feet could move me down that crawl.

So I called, and my brother answered,
years older, years taller, strong
shoulders and long arms stretching,
reaching my straining hands, my hands
in his, the rest of me coming naturally.

Years later my brother, in his quiet, dark
living room reached and fell,
his large, much older body tumbling
to the floor, silent on a carpet brown as hay,
leaving me nights I dream about long
arms reaching for a frightened boy

My Father's Hands

My hands I do not notice during winter.
The winter hands are always red,
the chapping like a second skin hands put on
to show they mean the manly life and do not quiver
in the harsh blast of snow and freezing rain.

This spring, though, the hands seem not
to have recovered. It is not just the long-lost touch
of softness, the smooth skin of youth, whose absence
startles. The brown spots have multiplied, the skin
a rasp that cannot smooth a board or face. Veins
seem darker, rivers of cold blood under ice. Quiet hands
that show no beauty except a golden ring that grows
as firmly fixed as the wrinkled knuckle just above it.

These are quiet hands now. I cannot read their palms,
but in the coarse and brown-marked skin,
in the blue rivers of blood, I see my father as I
once knew him, his large and gentle hands
in the hands of his son.

Climbing a Pine Tree

We climbed the huge, sprawling pine
that predated by a century the white, two-porched,
colonnaded house my ancestors bought when they
migrated from the deep South, where they fought
their brothers in the war of the states.
Older than the farm that gave life
to generations of my transplanted family,
it stretched back beyond the long vanished fort down
the road, to the last battles Indians fought
for survival in that part of the country.

That pine we climbed even before we could walk,
my mother holding a child like a doll
on a limb stretching out straight as an arm pointed
toward the west, toward the dazzling evening sun,
and the child barely able to hold his head up,
and the wind closing his eyes, slipping through hair,
in its way as gentle as the mother.

I came to that pine last, when my brothers had grown out
of that sort of climbing, and only my sister and I
still cared for it, she playing games of trees
with me because there was no other child her age.
By myself, when she went off to school,
I would stand in the center where three large shafts
grew up and out, and where I could grow tired
and lean backward without fear of falling.

Even in my best of days, I never climbed much higher.
It was not a tree for scaling heights,
for daring ventures, for risking arms and legs
to struggle far above one's reach. I would crawl out,
though, along that straight arm of a limb at times
and sit and balance and think of risks. Mainly,
though, I contented myself with the sturdy trunks
of things, hid out between my wooden trinity,
and prayed through small realities, like cones that grew
in multitudes, and that, if flung just right,
would whiz through air with just a trace of sound
and curve gracefully across the road, into the ditch.

Then grown, for years I would bring my children back
for climbing of their own. I would stand beside
the tree, my wife would peep through her small camera
and press a button, and we would add the photo
to the history of our children growing up.

Only now, when my children too have finished
climbing, I realize it was as much the tree's history
being written as our own. The long string of children
climbing this safe and sturdy tree
just proved true what I had suspected:
that there are things in this world that never change,
that dreams prove best that are thick and strong,
that wind loves better than human praying,
and what gives us most gives just by being.

I Keep the Water Flowing

I keep the water flowing all year in
the stock tank. It's a pleasure in spring,
except for the mud about the tank,
the barnyard mud, but even that's a sign
of good to come. The cold water flows
easily from hose to tank, and cows cooped up
too much strain and stretch black sagging necks
to reach the sweet clear stream.

In summer I stock the tank, delighting
in my pun, with bullheads taken from
a neighbor's brook where it flows along
the gravel road, under the bridge.
They keep to the bottom, avoiding as best
they can the looming, cavernous mouths.
They float still at noon, pick up
speed when shadows fall across the sky.
They fare well in summer, adapting to
their green-walled world.

Most make it to the fall. Those that don't,
swooped up in cow suction, unlike Jonah
in the belly of a whale, don't return
to tell their stories. As fall drops by,
the cold nips the corners of their world.
They grow sluggish. The cows drink less.
The water threatens to cross the line from
flowing stream to stagnant pool. We know
that death is coming.

One by one, the bullheads float to the top,
belly-up. With a wide grain shovel I pluck
them from the surface before freeing the cattle
from their stanchions. Later, when I must break
the ice with spade or, when cold reaches to my
bones, with ax, I have almost forgotten fish
and concentrate on the slow Holsteins shaking
their heat against the air, and hurry to open
up the water's surface. The water tastes
like fire, I imagine, but perhaps with a twinge
of bullhead seasoning.

Forecasting

They talk weather down
out of the sky, Jack leaning back
against the door of his pick-up,
elbows denting
the thin blue metal,
one heel hooked on the running board.
Henry, hands in pockets, stands straight
as a denim flagpole.

Spring rain starts crops at their call,
humidity pulls the corn higher,
tassels it out. Fall drops
ripe pumpkins after the last haying,
glazes corncribs with the first frost.
Winter locks the world in white.

They talk it all down, then go
their ways, scorning TV forecasters,
certain of their own roles
in the cosmic order.

The Ear Hears, Though

The farm, when I return, has changed almost
beyond recognition, buildings caving in to time,
fields in ten-year set-aside, the only animals
small shapes in weeds, fireflies, birds too
quiet, bats swooping in black.

The ear hears, though,
timeless as sky:
> the steady drone of the motor
> for the milking machines, lulling
> cows to quiet, their heavy bodies
> patient, slow cud-chewing, tails
> swishing flies as if disconnected
> from their bodies, appendages
> as isolated as if they too were
> run by the motor hanging on a
> wooden ledge from the ceiling,
> wisps of graying hay caught
> in its thick black grease;

> stanchions rattling now, late in
> the evening, patience wearing
> thin, the last cows anxious
> for release into the darkened
> barnyard, then the slow walk down
> the dirt lane into the night
> pasture, ready for easy grazing
> under moon and stars, wind in
> the dark cornfields, rustling
> of long green leaves the sweet
> lullaby of solace for cow ears

that I hear now, years and miles between
the past and present, a divide as heavy as a
thick barn door, as porous as the strainer pad
that removed debris from the warm, sweet milk
that was each cow's reason for living, lifeblood
of the farm, part of the smoothly flowing river
of my life echoing down distant, hidden channels.

Like A Painting

The sun just risen
over the cold-blanched hills,
cows shuffling in place
in the steaming barn
and an invisible rooster
reckoning the time,

my father walked slowly
from the silent, sleeping house
across the snow-covered driveway,
my child's boots following his tracks.
He lay down in the cow barn
on a small bed of dried hay
in an empty pen,

pushed with his hands
against the rupture that pulled
pain through him
like a rasp dragging
across a face,

then lifted himself
up, right hand grasping
a stout board on the calves' manger,
and proceeded with the milking,
the cows giving forth
their meager winter servings
of warm milk
into the tall cold pail,

all the time pain hanging
its cruel presence on my father,
like the frozen sun on top
of a frozen hill, like a painting
hanging on a wall
in the house of my childhood.

The Sweet Odor of Corn Silage

He threw the silage down in forkfuls
piled high, the wide-spread tines

holding green fodder in chunks and the thin
crusts off silo walls. When he finished,

he crawled backward out the opening, leaving
the wooden door against an inside wall,

and came down carefully, facing inward, work
shoes pressing, fingers grasping the rungs,

stepping at the bottom into the silage pile.
Later, when his wife did the washing,

she had to shake silage out of the cuffs
of his overalls, and out of pockets.

Even today, I cannot think of him in his bib
overalls without smelling the sweet odor of silage.

Out of the Blue

Lightning snaked down out
of the lone dark cloud
in the blue sky. Heat crackled
in the hay, two gray horses
stood still, like granite, frozen
in the awesome moment.

The thin boy forking hay
from the hay loader to corners
of the load felt the surge
of electricity like blood through
his body. He felt a falling,
then nothing. The hay caught
him, dust and sweat coating
his skin. The other workers said
they could smell a burning then,
and saw a puff of smoke when he
was struck. My father helped unload
him, men gentler than women
laid him softly on a piece of
canvas someone found. He looked
so young, they said, in death.

A somber procession brought
him back from that far field
in an empty wagon he would
have filled with winter feed
for cows now waiting out
the bitter heat under a clump
of trees in a pasture the men
passed by. As they turned a corner
women in the kitchen saw
the coming and rushed to meet
who it was, each one fearing,
each with the hope that bears
the guilt of wanting death
for someone else. "Oh, God, not
him!" The bearers brought the boy
through the kitchen and into
the parlor, where, reverent as in church,
they placed him on the floor.

Before Bone

Eve wept.
The bells of her body clanged
and the tulips learned an elemental longing,
having heard this first song.

There are moments in which the whip of her voice
travels to us. Now, for example, city sounds converging
behind St. Paul's Cathedral - car horns and church bells
marking the evening commute.

Oh, to have known that first leap
from the trees. Her hands sifting through
the creation of ash. What she saw
in the layers, that opening - of - a - wound,
must have made an enormous sound.

Travelogue

I took a train that ran through fields and ended up at the sun.
No one would believe me though I had the scents to prove it. I wore
each pore-deep. First I smelled of wheat burning, done
in by smoke that choked the hideouts where older boys went to score.

No one would believe me though I had the sense to prove it. I wore
ribbons in my hair, which birds mistook for rivers, following me
into the hideouts where older boys went to score.
I saw the ribbons later, tucked into nests high in the trees.

I wore ribbons in my hair, which birds mistook for rivers. Boys followed me
but lost interest. It was easy to read their bodies through grain dust.
I could see the ribbons later, tucked into nests high in the trees.
For so long, afraid of seeing, flying was a must.

Soon I lost interest. I couldn't read my own palm through the dust.
Time passed slowly as other girls got breasts, locked themselves in
bathrooms for so long, afraid of seeing that flying was no longer a must.
In bathrooms girls made their faces look like Queen Nefertiti in her tomb.

Time passed slowly as other girls got breasts and hid in bathrooms.
I was lovely at night, thinking the stars made
all the other girls look like Queen Nefertiti withering in her tomb.
My dreams were silence and dust, braided.

I felt lovely only at night, thinking the stars had made
me dream of silence and dust, pore-deep. I smelled the wheat, done
in by threshers that redefined the field's subtle grade.
I took a train that ran through fields and ended up at the sun.

Not Knowing

Ask the right question
and I'll give you a star:

It is a lighthouse hidden by incoming
waves. It promises cure

like the hand of Christ.
Is it a dark slate of courage?

I wished to be fearless. But
instead you get the galaxy

with its desperate temper,
the moon strange and yearning

as we are. Take it.
It shines a beautiful fraction.

My Father Waking

A tough belief bruised my sleep:
that I might wake to find our whole house empty,
the remains of daily life - dishes, coloring books,
my mother's red scarf - charred beyond recognition.

That prospect wavered in stars
across the ceiling, ruining the sleep I needed.
A dog cut the night with its bark, in an effort
to speak what in human terms

becomes the sharp fall through air, our imprint kissed
on rock below. My father's snore hissed past
each window, in a heat so intense
it surprised the frogs out of singing.

There was a boxcar in which our voices were kept:
it snaked through alfalfa fields, throwing sudden halos
over unwashed pots and pans. His face in the bottom of a glass,
where it stayed for days. Full of chalk when he woke.

What songs came from that slumber? Surrendering to sleep,
I dreamt my father into the midnight glare - pointing a gun
at the dog whose legs barely make it off the ground
before the shot aroused the entire town.

Karaoke

Through smoke and mirrors -
over *Copacabana* or Elvis remixed - people
manage small talk. Girls this season are sporting

baby-tees and glitter for their cleavage,
ogling the cowboy with a belt buckle
half the size of his head.
And from the back of the bar

contestant number seven looks like
she's headed toward stardom, though later
her head will get rammed
through the window of a Dodge parked outside.

She doesn't know, crooning to Patsy Cline,
sequined fingernails wrapped around the mike,
how good it will feel to hit the snow covered ground.

Hurricane Season
For Steve

The smell of coming rain
overwhelms the air.

The kudzu trumpets
through iron gates, undone
while I wait for
the rattle of your keys.

One colorless bloom scattering
its ineffable script on the porch.
Tomorrow this ink will be dry,
boats at the riverfront
still scraping the pier.

Coincidence

Once, day vanished while I was sitting in traffic
and I couldn't remember how to drive.

Exhaust and horizon met in a line of smoke
lifting over car hoods - language finally given

tangible shape. It seemed a script for living right,
but its vowels refused to return for translation.

All I could decipher was: *December is the different
shadows a bare tree casts on stone.*

Not familiar with natural history, I wept. The sun continued
going down, and at first I dreamed

it meant there was more time for stars. Coming back
to my body, I realized it meant nothing at all.

Blizzard

Invisible, drunk on wine, an arid bluster.
There is time. It has a voice and moves
slowly. Let's just say you go
three days without human touch
and no one at the grocery store
tries to make eye contact.

You live in a city of Gloucesters,
but here's your name on a list. Are you ink,
or less permanent? Once you saw the mountain
and it meant something clear. Conquerable.

The Other Desert

I suffer because I want.

For a buzzard to circle, a place on the farthest continent
to call home. All roads have disappeared

and the starlet birch buzzes as the wind dies down,

before churchgoers caravan across two-lane stretches,
home to a cold fireplace and lights left on in rooms

where the television brings the desert out of memory.

What is it that holds us to it - sand becoming glass?
Heat that drives back even the stars? The other desert is the space

between what I imagine and what is actual - browns fading to more

brown, a body broken through to its bones and rotting
in the asphalt dark, the soot-thick hush of every lived-in town.

Making the Harp

It is distance I sometimes crave.
Few things praise the body more. My shape
an absence - no: a cathedral, humming.
Starless night, sky split open
with pines and the world left unsolved
by its necessary trespasses -
burnt - out flowers in a ditch,
the smell of their dying
a kind of rain. I had wanted to begin
in the other story, where a woman
finds the print of her lover's shoe
after the tomatoes have died.
The way her hands
sought the edge of the dirt
is also a story. I don't know how to answer:
only that there is a train plowing
through every harvest sleep
and a man who spun like wheat
toward a woman he loved.
Could have saved her,
but refused. Wanting to make audible
the deepest harp he possessed.

Red River

One drought summer, a horse's head appeared
across the sandbar, mouth flung open to water,
teeth preserved in the river's iron muck.

Arrowheads flanked brittle banks, worn
to the same sheenless gray of late summer leaves
falling onto the bridge, where we considered

the horse's fate: its ghost trailing us
as we rode bicycles and played spin-the-bottle
behind grain storage bins. The fields kept to themselves,

cradling sunburnt farmhands who cursed and kicked
crops never gone to seed. Those same men later
untied two neighbor boys swinging from rafters -

their dried blood mingled with a barn swallow's blood:
the bird had flown into the traps hung like gauntlets
throughout the gutted rick. There were seas

wheat-colored and irreverent, stalks quaking
as the funeral procession headed out of town. No one
could look away from their tides, just as we could not turn our heads

when we'd opened the barn doors, finding
the boys, their skin the color of clouds
that later brought torrential rain.

The Lantern

Keep walking through the flames:
                     On a yellow post-it note.

Don't hate me for my absence:
                     Everyone I've considered falling in love with.

It's not for lack of want: What did you want?

**

I still remember the small of your back
but I am happy you're getting married: Was that one written down?

I never sent you a letter
but when I saw your handwriting
my own hands shook:
                     I can no longer play the piano.

**

Wonderful to hear you are not dead. Will you wait
until I pass to send a bunch of hollyhocks
a season past their prime?

**

There was a night we walked the edge
of the only highway out of town.
That was another kind of love. And the moon
was a lantern: who held it then?

Gypsy Red

I know that red had nothing to do with his death.
It's mere accident, an idea with consequence.

Summers after, I watched Mrs. D
peering out the window, insulted
that life would continue

despite a husband buried
and the cat not home since July.
Evenings she called "Ginger"

over and over: a neighborhood joke
like the time her son swam naked
in the municipal pool, claiming
to have sleepwalked through it all.

Ten years later he drove to Kansas
and hung himself in a hotel room,
wallet emptied by the housekeeper
and family photos taken out

with last night's trash. His fingernails
were painted gypsy red.

Most of us lack the follow-through,
as the small towns we're born into
might lack charm, save Mrs. D
who paints her nails long into night.
Her hands form a truce
with the Kansas prairie she's never seen.

She locks her fingers together -
which make a temple or a prison
and hold the scent of curtains
slightly moved for a better view of the road.

Devotions: Two Views

A.

I lied about the angel.
My grandmother made me do it -
the tape recorder on, her palsied hand
suspended like a hummingbird
over my head. *Tell me about
the spirit.* About something holy
entering you. I thought if I told her
the angel was dressed in pink
she would minister to me with kisses -
a blessing like the church elders pouring olive oil
over her head. The lie anointed,
we began the first morning prayer.

B.

About the angel she lied. On the tape recorder,
her voice: *she appeared in a dream
about the spirit, who was pink.*
They were blushing from the holy lie.
The wings, too - but shredded
like cooked flesh falling
from the bone. The grandmother's hands
were shaking like they might take off.
Did the grandmother make her do it?
She wanted to read from the *Book of Mormon.*
Anything for the oil. Anointing the lie,
they spoke the first morning prayer.

Late November

The final blossoms forging their yellow music -
grace notes swinging through polluted air. A door still rings
on its hinges. Down the sun-worn streets sirens shout
through every chance to dream. Let us approximate

the rural silence of bridges slicked with snow,
a makeshift roof over stubborn shoots of clover.
Sleep beginning as wheat undulated across the plains, toward

tractor tires abandoned. Their tread loosened to dust.
Do not mistake this for pleasure. This is where
I build an immovable image,
cold silos the only compass toward home.

Wanderlüst

The American frontier lost its flavor years ago,
but you keep traveling farther west, our conversations
stilted by mountain ranges, the radio's endless
spin of Willie & Waylon tunes. The ride home

is a long one, and during it you read the landscape
for signs of this discernable hymn: we may not endure.
Newspaper headlines curling to dust,
rolling from one coast to the other, beyond

booze bottles hurled into ditches, the glow
of your Marlboros smoked two at a time. What is there
to say above the din of the desert? That time once felt
like something you could hold in your hands, when it was

cold enough to watch our breath rise and move
through the air, ahead of the next adventure? Are you still
following that line - toward an end with some unsolvable
longing? Send word as soon as you arrive.

Blue Ice

~ For Betsy

After years, the stiff skates still slip on over wool socks.
White laces intersect and climb
up our ankles
until the geometry is complete
with a double bow.

I follow you onto the shoveled ice.
My legs wobble and dull blades hesitate.
You have been practicing and push and glide
with ease while I stutter behind you.

Then, as the crisp surface cleans my blades,
I match your pace, almost, and once again
we are gliding across this disk of ice
as many years ago, stroking the lake
with our stride, leaving behind
a wake of ice chips.

We avoid the hem of blue ice, feel
the winter air sting our cheeks and noses.
The sky is bold and bright and we
are skating again. Not even darkness
will sadden us tonight.

Tattoo: New Orleans

For freshman girls living in Newcomb Hall,
tattoos were especially bad,
when Liza McBride and I took the trolley
to the French Quarter, continued on foot
down seedy Esplanade Ave
past drunks swigging beer,
smoking grass on street corners
and we marched right into the first tattoo parlor
we could find open at 4:00 on a Friday afternoon.

Daring Scorpios, we were celebrating
our 18th birthdays far from home;
me from "Live Free or Die"
New Hampshire where such expression
was not legal for young girls, and Liza
from Troy, New York, home of Uncle Sam,
and a hippie mom who gave her permission.

Inside the parlor, decals on the walls illustrated our options:
skulls and cross bones, Celtic crosses, a devil,
the ubiquitous Harley Davidson banner.
The girl behind the counter was painting her nails pink,
humming to Dolly Parton, *"How y'all doing?"* she drawled.

From the smaller display on the counter,
Liza choose a rose, and I, a butterfly,
left shoulders, on the back, where showing would be optional.
Liza went first - I held her hand as the woman etched
petals into Liza's shoulder, added the red bloom, the green
of stem and leaf. I was next. It felt like the sharp edge
of a tweezer carving into my back, the sting of a yellow jacket.

After, with hand mirrors, we inspected her work.
"Y'all happy?" We were. She gave us salve, band-aids,
we gave her twenty dollars each. She put the bills in her back
jeans pocket, and confessed,
"Y'all know, those the first tattoos I've done."

We didn't know, nor care,
but went to the Old Absinthe bar, ordered Bailey's Irish Cream
over ice and toasted our new tattoos.

That summer, my father would swat my shoulder,
thinking he was killing a deer fly, and my mother
would shake her head, beyond words.
Years later, I tried to find Liza McBride,
now a registered nurse, according to my alumni magazine,
a mother of two in Hudson, New York, but she never answered
my letters.

Now, my tattoo is a dull blob, it looks more
like the state of Rhode Island than a butterfly.
Still, when I think of our trolley ride back to Newcomb Hall,
checking our band-aids to make sure blood didn't stain
our blouses, in a place so far away from home it could have been Tahiti,
I still feel the sting of wings on my shoulder,
the flutter and pulse of youth.

Summer Sunday

At slack tide a man walks in water,
knee deep waves cloud all around him
like windy sky.
Beach tents and striped umbrellas
shelter napping toddlers and sunburnt
tourists with white noses and shaded eyes.
Sandwiches come out of coolers
without glances at watches,
and gulls wait for their picnic share,
laughing.

Sunday comics and book reviews flap
in the afternoon east wind, as shadows grow.
Greenheads are now hunted and swatted with
ferocity, and parents take their sea tossed children
home to garden hoses and hamburgers on the grill.

The sky gets thinner
as the tide rises higher.
The last few towels are moved away
from the shoreline and shaken. They snap
like laundry in the evening air.
The beach wears
the incoming tide like a bed sheet,
and Sunday fades
like a long, deep breath.

Off Shore, Becalmed

Waves slowly swell,
clouds cling to the horizon,
the air is stubborn, still.
No dolphins follow us,
no schools of fish.
We float in an immense embrace of blue.
The mast groans, the sails sputter.

A box bobs ahead
wrapped with red twine
like a Christmas gift.
Cautiously we circle,
stingy with our limited fuel,
yet starving for distraction.
The boat hook catches the rope
like a gardener's hoe
pulling up a weed,
and we haul in the treasure
of soggy newspapers, Styrofoam.

Salt. Water. Sun.
We listen to the shortwave
radio, coast guard reports,
static and silence.
Three days of flat water.

We are not discoverers.
All land has been claimed
and reclaimed, flags are hung.
We just want to deliver this boat
to her port of call, and to step again
on terra firma, to have a drink
of fresh water, to watch the sun
set over land.
But now we drift on, looking for continents
in the clouds, waiting for wind.

Funeral

I am driving to the funeral
of my childhood friend's father.
She and I never thought we'd meet like this
when we were eleven, braiding
our ponies' manes, practicing
canters with our eyes closed.

I arrive early and walk the beach.
The sea sparkles in the morning sunlight,
air is crisp as fresh linen, the waves celebrate
their arrival to shore. I pick a pebble
to remember this moment.
At the service, sadness presses down on me

in the organ's Alleluia, the Meditation Hymn,
the Prayers of Final Commendation.
My grief takes me by surprise
among the restrained mourners.
After, when I hear your voice
across the reception room,

it's as though we're teenagers again, as though
I'd been hearing it all these years since
we waited for our periods, wore our first bras,
smoked cigarettes on the sea wall,
lied about our ages, we so wanted
to be older.

Now, we embrace, wipe tears.
We're best friends again
though now we've grown up
and your father has died,
and one day mine will too.

How do we learn to lose
our parents? Not the way we lost our childhood, which
we couldn't wait to shed, or young adulthood,
which we lost without even knowing.
Now we want to grasp every moment,
though now we know we cannot.

Muscle Memory

If the muscles remember
every wrap and release, how
they must mourn the loss of love,
and time spent loving.

What widow does not ache
for her husband's hips to embrace -
What former rider forgets
the pulse of trot beneath her -
What retired sailor doesn't yearn
for the sea's swell, its surge
of surf and tide?

Does muscle memory also hold a place
for anticipation? For fear?
Or, is she like her sister, Cognition,
that once she changes her mind
can no longer remember
her original position?

Like the amputee who still feels
the impulsion of his phantom legs,
this memory is far more honest
than intellect, more loyal
to our bodies, than our brain is
to our fickle minds.

Old Mare

Rain rot on your fetlocks,
withers, and back. Your neck is tender with arthritis,
your teeth have grown too long to chew.
Thin hipped, weak hocked, the scar in your right eye
may be from a hoof, a boot, a belt.
Still you retain your kind eyes, quiet pools of mahogany.
You nestle your starred forehead against my cheek.

The horse dealer promotes you:
Bomb proof, anyone can ride, dead
calm, I kid you not.
12 years old, new shoes, a real
bargain.

Yet, your tattooed lip dates you: 1975,
Waco, Texas. Prized Melody.
You started thirteen races
at age three, three times you placed.
And then? Twenty four years of mystery.

The vet shakes her head: *This aged mare*
shows decades of neglect. In all honesty,
worth the price at the rendering factory,
79 cents a pound. Yet she deserves much more.

Daily I curry off the rot, douse
your sores with iodine, dress your scabs.
Soon, your bay coat shines like a polished
chestnut, your stiff neck loosens,
and you canter like a filly when I call.

Old mare,
your kind eye is rewarded.
You have grass and grain to round your ribbed belly,
little girls to braid your mane, put sparkles on your starred forehead,
and whisper your name before they go to sleep, Prized Melody.

Taking Shelter: Puerto Plata

At the Hotel Castilla
a pale pink mosquito net
hangs over the bed,
like an awning from a ballerina's leftover mesh.
The rain plays itself on the drooping gutters.

Shuttered windows gape out.
They are yellow, the yellow of faded
foul weather jackets, weathered buoys.
A varnished mahogany table
graces the corner, a bird
of paradise rests in a jar.

Water now gushes off the lip of roof,
seeps in under the balcony doors,
soaking the floorboards.
The streets have become
soft brown canals,
clogged with plastic wrappers,
banana peels, a dead kitten.
The storm drains flush up
all our traces
onto sidewalks and doorways.

Something so pure and sad
and inevitable.
The dye has run from my sandals,
my toes are rust red.
The sea coughs up seaweed,
driftwood, and tin cans,
iridescent as mermaid gills.

Family Dinners Out

Once a year we ate out, always at Jerry's Restaurant.
From our house, we could almost see the building on the marsh
which we tasted in the water, *Low tide water* we would call it,
and plead for the rare occasion to drink Coke
served in giant glasses with striped straws which bent near the top.

We had the largest table to fit all seven of us, plus my parents
who sat at opposite ends to spread out adult supervision.
We ate fried clams, dripping with catsup, heaps
of French fries, a few obligatory pokes at coleslaw
and baskets full of rolls, refilled. "They're included in the price,"

my mother reminded us, and we always got our money's worth.
Any leftover she wrapped in a napkin and put in her purse
for breakfast in the morning, along with wrapped pats of butter
served on a plate with a cube of ice.

And although I was usually too full, we were allowed to order dessert.
My brothers indulged in ice cream sundaes
in scalloped glasses, strawberries and fudge rippling through
the vanilla until it was mashed into one color of mud and slurped
with long spoons - the kind of behavior never allowed
at the table at home, but at Jerry's
my parents looked away.

Afterward, we would pile into the station wagon and drive home,
our bellies aching, the smell of warm rolls wafting
from my mother's full purse.

Holy Places

In the iglesia Ponce de Lyon,
the sunlight is dusty, it drifts in
from high arched windows, darkened
from candles, incense smoke.
Spanish hymns scratch from speakers
dangling over the pulpit.
Cobwebbed porticos
shelter the assembled saints,
St. Stephen smiling at the ceiling,
Peter and John standing in a dory,
arms stretched out as if for balance.
The Virgin Mary looks dazed,
her green eyes stare blankly
as a slippery hooked fish.
Around her feet lie lilies
brown as old asparagus.
The flowers cover
a serpent's pointed head.
No one minds the collection box,
the postcards, prayer candles,
the strings of rosary beads.
Tour groups come only on Saturday.

Outside, vendors sell crushed ice,
cured beef, bamboo flutes.
The grass has been blessed with rain.
In the hills, where the air is hushed,
sugar cane bows to the sky.

Explanations, After Meeting Your Parents

Late one night
you told me
how the fascists came,
shot Henri in the back
while your grandmother
crouched across the room.

She had hidden your mother
with the preserves until the men rode away.
Then, she dragged Henri's body out
behind the chicken coop,
covered it with lumps of snow,
bloodied red, she said,
as a rooster's comb.

It was January. She wrapped her feet
in wool, carried her daughter
into the mountains, headed north.
Her feet turned blue and her soles cracked
but she could not feel them.
When she reached the French border,
she heard church bells ringing
and she thought she had died.
To this day, she walks on her heels,
speaks Italian in her sleep.

Your mother married young,
an indecisive graying priest.
He left the Church, but never
left her, although you say
he should have, long ago.
They sleep separately now
and share breakfast like strangers.
He drinks red wine each night
to rinse away his guilt.
Alone, she attends Mass,
thanks God for her perfect sons,
her beautiful feet, her safe home,
for her life, far more
than was ever promised to be.

In the All Night Laundromat

I wash my sheets at dawn.
The air is muggy, milky white.
Across the street, a thin man
sways out of Tyler's Jazz Garden
with a Dixie beer in his hand.
He tipped me a ten for a $2.50 tab
only a few hours ago.
Now, he does a little two step
on the curb, gracefully bows
to no one, and sashays away.

A woman comes in through the place
where a door belongs.
Her face is stitched in
like a nylon stocking doll.
A brown baby rests on her hip,
a green garbage bag of laundry
slung over her shoulder.
She looks at me,
at the wooden benches,
then at the huge broken window
where a Pontiac ended up last week.
We are alone in the world
of soap and water.

I warn her, that first machine is busted,
takes your change, then won't spin.
"*Honey,*" she says, "*I know
all about it,*" pointing with her hip,
baby and all. "*Don't feed that one a dime,
that one there, it works for nothin.*"

Taking Down the House

My husband relishes the crowbar,
he pulls off the wall's housedress of plaster
as if it were diseased,
unprys the ribs of lath that wave across
the rooms from post to beam,
and celebrates the new open space.

As I shovel the rubble of once wall,
I find clumps of sorrel, shards of clam shell.
One hundred and fifty years ago, someone
mixed this plaster. Who gathered these clams
and ground their shells? Whose mare
or gelding shed this winter coat, was it curried
as forsythia bloomed? Did it line the nests
of house wrens and robins?

In the kitchen, layers of wallpaper.
A woman hung each roll, I imagine a Rosa,
choosing the blue floral pattern one spring,
replacing it years later with the American Eagle
after woodsmoke had grayed the kitchen garden.
I see her kneading bread by the window,
stoking the stubborn woodstove fire,
scrubbing the weekly wash.
I wish we could sit down together, share a cup of tea,
talk about the best way to cook fiddleheads,
make mulberry jam, clean out a well.

The wrenched lath and crumbled plaster
makes me feel sick and sorrow
for this solid house. I hope it will forgive us.
If these rooms could speak, they might share
a birthing story, a wake. They might teach us
about time, what matters, or doesn't.

At day's end the tiny kitchen joins the dining room
and becomes one. We sit in the debris
banking the center chimney, rest our weary backs on the proud brick.
I think of Rosa, her wallpaper, her recipes.
I forgive my husband, his joy of destruction.
We will settle, like the dust.

Mud

It takes a long winter
to appreciate mud
season, which has arrived in ruts
and rivulets along the driveway and
back roads where I travel home.

The smell of wet dirt is pure
and forbidden. Something so primal
in that earthen ooze, it squishes and sucks
as I slosh through it in my L.L. Bean boots,
it splashes and spits on my pant legs,
it covers my little economy car.

After a deep thaw, water will soak down
into the earth where we need it.
Come summer, missing our mud, we'll fill
watering cans, unwind garden hoses,
and we'll make it again.

Humming to Snails
~ For Anne

Landlocked
among hills spotted with cattle,
valleys of leafy silo corn,
I return home
to the scent of salt, the grit of sand,
the songs of gulls and sea pipers,
to hum to the snails.

Did you know
if you hold a snail in the palm of your hand
and hum, stopping only to breathe when needed,
the snail will crawl out of his shell
and visit you? Stop
the hum, and he will slide back into his home
leaving you only the reflection
of his winking eye.

This I learned from my mother,
and how to count the age of seaweed,
the bitter taste of beach mustard,
where to find a mermaid's purse.
How to parse the grammar of the sea
and the syntax of her shore,
the symmetry of a mussel shell,
so milky blue,
so pure, so fine.

THE POETS

Ted Bookey moved to Maine in 1980 from New York, where he taught English in public school and at Long Island University. He teaches modern American poetry and Shakespeare in the Senior College at the University of Maine in Augusta. He is the author of two poetry books, <u>Mixty Motions</u> and, in collaboration with his wife Ruth, a book of translations of Erich Kastner. His poetry, criticisms and reviews appear in many journals and anthologies. "I believe in the comic vision—poetry never lost anything by having both feet on the ground, one on a banana peel."

Jay Davis lives in Portland, where he has been reading and appearing in the spoken word/slam poetry scene for the last 10 years. His work has been published in Café Review, Monkey's Fist, and several small 'zines. He has been a featured reader at poetry venues in Bridgewater and Cambridge, MA, Portsmouth, NH and many places in Maine. During the day, he works as a computer database specialist. <u>Whispers, Cries & Tantrums</u> is his first chapbook.

Jay Franzel lives in Wayne, Maine with his daughter and their dingo. He has worked with at-risk students for twenty years, currently teaching in Winthrop. His poems have been published in Café Review and other journals. <u>Walking Track</u> is his first chapbook.

Nancy A. Henry has published hundreds of poems in journals and online 'zines. She has been nominated four times for a Pushcart Prize and won an Atlanta Review International Merit Award. She teaches part-time at Southern Maine Community College, and works as patient rights liaison at Spring Harbor Hospital in Westbrook. She has had many careers, including attorney in the child protection field. Her chapbooks are <u>Brie Fly</u>, <u>Anything Can Happen</u>, <u>Hard</u>, <u>Eroslon</u> and <u>Europe on $5 A Day</u>. She and Alice met in law school in 1983 and a mere twenty years later, started Moon Pie Press.

Michael Macklin, of Portland, works as a carpenter. He is reviews editor of Café Review and received an MFA in Writing from Vermont College this year. His poetry has appeared in various journals including Animus and Rattle. <u>Driftland</u> is his first chapbook.

Robin Merrill was born and lives in Farmington, Maine with the man of her dreams and their bloodhound. She is a 1999 graduate of Maine Maritime Academy and worked in the Merchant Marine for several years. Her poems have appeared in over a hundred publications, and she has several chapbooks. Visit her at www.robinmerrill.com.

David Moreau lives in Wayne, Maine with his wife, son and daughter. He works in Lewiston with developmentally disabled adults. He is the author of another chapbook, <u>Children are Ugly Little Monsters (But You Have to Love Them Anyway)</u>. David's poems have appeared in many journals, and he is active in the Maine poetry reading scene.

Alice Persons lives in Westbrook with her collection of pets. She works for a legal publisher, teaches part time at the University of Southern Maine, and volunteers for the Animal Refuge League of Greater Portland. <u>Be Careful What You Wish For</u> was her first chapbook; <u>Never Say Never</u> was her second. Her poetry has appeared in Animus, Aurorean, Off the Coast, and other journals.

Ed Rielly grew up on a dairy farm in Wisconsin and came to Maine 27 years ago. He is the chair of the English department at St. Joseph's College in Windham. Ed and his wife Jeanne have two children and three grandchildren. His previous publications include nine poetry chapbooks, four nonfiction books, and book reviews. He is currently completing a biography of F. Scott Fitzgerald and a collection of essays on teaching baseball across the college curriculum.

Darcy Shargo, who lives in Augusta, has an MFA from Goddard College. She has a background in teaching, technical writing and program management. She and her husband Steve recently welcomed their first child. <u>The Flame and the Fiction</u> is her first chapbook.

Ellen Taylor teaches writing and literature at the University of Maine in Augusta. She has her husband Daniel live in Appleton, Maine with their hound dog Mack and a horse called Noble Esperanza. Ellen's work has appeared in numerous journals, including Puckerbrush and North American Review. <u>Humming to Snails</u> was her first chapbook; she also has one, <u>Letters from the Third World</u>, from Sheltering Pines Press.